Praise for *The Myth of Meditation*

Paramananda's latest book has ~~~~~~ ~~~~~ out of a ~~~~~~~ ~~~~~ :tice and engagement. It is beautiful ~~~~~~~~~~~~~~~ ~tle, sensitive and poetic meeting of o  ; of a cliché to say it speaks both to be~ ~~~~~~~~~ ~~~~~)rs alike, I can't speak for beginners, t~ ~~~~~~~~~~~~~~~~~~ ~~~~ued of another great meditation teacher - ~~~~~~ ~uzuki, and his famous book *Zen Mind, Beginner's Mind.* Paramananda is able to encourage us to the openness of the beginner's mind, drawing the reader back to their own experience, giving them enough instruction and encouragement to be with the elusive, the understated, the difficult. This book will help you find your way back to your own vulnerable heart, connected to the mythic heart of the world.

– **Jayaraja,** Chair of Buddhafield, author of
The Yellow Book of Games and Energizers

This is a critical and necessary book to read, to practise and to embody. Brilliant in its depth and simplicity, Paramananda allows meditation to become poetry, to return to its so-called original face. This return to origins filled my eyes with tears of sadness about the world around us and at the same time utter joyfulness in the refuge of such a poetic heart inside us all. Thank you to Paramananda for writing this book.

Michael Shea, PhD, meditation teacher
and founder of sheaheart.com

In this book Paramananda beautifully examines how spiritual practice is both a deeply intimate relationship with oneself, and inextricably connected to the world we live in. He weaves nature, ecology, myth, poetry and philosophy through his narrative, into imaginative and enlivening meditative exercises. He brings far-reaching Buddhist teachings down to earth and encourages us to be curious, as we simply sit with the breathing body, or open to suffering – our own and others' – in such a way that liberates the heart.

Paramananda has a distinctive 'voice' that is original, unruffled and wise. He draws on his considerable experience as a teacher and writer of Buddhism over many years. His decades of practice shine through, with each word richly communicating warmth, confidence and authenticity.

Vajradevi, meditation teacher and
author of uncontrivedmindfulness.net

The Myth of Meditation

Restoring imaginal ground through embodied Buddhist practice

Paramananda

Windhorse Publications

Windhorse Publications
17e Sturton Street
Cambridge CB1 2SN
United Kingdom
info@windhorsepublications.com
windhorsepublications.com

Typeset and designed by Ruth Rudd
Cover design by Dhammarati. Cover image courtesy of Vidyadipa.
Printed by Bell & Bain Ltd, Glasgow

British Library Cataloguing in Publication Data:
A catalogue record for this book is available from the British Library

ISBN: 978-1-911407-21-8

Contents

About the author

Paramananda was born John Wilson in north London in 1955. From an early age he was curious about Eastern ideas, but it was not until the age of twenty-three, after the death of his father, that his interest in Buddhism was aroused. At this time, the focus of his life shifted from the world of politics, in which he had been active, to more spiritual concerns.

Throughout his twenties, Paramananda worked mostly as a psychiatric social worker. He has also been involved in various types of voluntary work, including the Samaritans, drug detox, and more recently in a hospice.

In 1983 he came into contact with the Triratna Buddhist Order and, two years later, was ordained within the Order itself. Since then he has been teaching meditation and Buddhism full time in San Francisco and in London, where he now lives. He sees meditation and Buddhism as power tools for both individual and social change, and believes that service to the community is a vital aspect of spiritual practice.

Paramananda is the author of *Change Your Mind: A Practical Guide to Buddhist Meditation* (2005), *The Body* (2007), and *A Deeper Beauty* (2002), all published by Windhorse Publications.

Author's acknowledgements

Many thanks to Lucy Shaw for her help with the proofreading and organization of this book.

Publisher's acknowledgements

Windhorse Publications wishes to gratefully acknowledge a grant from the Triratna European Chairs' Assembly Fund and the Future Dharma Fund towards the production of this book. Windhorse Publications also wishes to gratefully acknowledge and thank the individual donors who gave to the book's production via our 'Sponsor-a-book' campaign.

Audio downloads

This book has been produced with accompanying guided meditations and reflections by the author, available as free downloads. They are marked with a 🧘, and can be streamed directly from the Web or downloaded in MP3 format.

Please go to: bit.ly/MythOfMeditationAudio or windhorsepublications.com/myth-of-meditation-audio.

Introduction

The intention of this book is to restore meditation to the 'imaginal ground' from which it arose. I do not mean this in a historical sense but rather a psychological one. This metaphorical ground resists literalization and upholds what I see as the fundamentally poetic nature of mindfulness in particular and meditation in general.

Mindfulness has always been at the heart of all Buddhist meditation practices. Most of the time, I will use the term 'meditation' rather than the term 'mindfulness' to distinguish it from the increasing number of secular uses of mindfulness – as a tool to manage pain or stress, or for any number of other benefits mindfulness can deliver, according to a growing body of recent research. Beneficial though these might be for specific contexts, I want to rescue meditation as it is defined in Buddhism from this quasi-medical/scientific framework of mindfulness in which it now risks being subsumed. The presentation of mindfulness as somehow separate from meditation can risk cutting it off from its origins and from its poetic and archetypal roots, and reduce it to a technique rather than seeing it as a way of being.

This book has emerged from my own practice and teaching of meditation over the last thirty years. I was ordained as a Buddhist in 1985, and since that time my life has been intimately connected with the teaching of meditation. I have taught in a wide variety of settings, from idyllic country retreats to city jails, hospices, and rehabilitation units, and most of all at urban Buddhist centres, mainly in London and San Francisco. My teaching has always been based in the Buddhist tradition. What I have tried to do is find a language in which this tradition becomes intelligible and inspiring to those of us living today.

This restating is in line with the history of Buddhism, which has constantly renewed itself through the ages, finding new forms of expression that are appropriate to the diverse cultures in which it has, in the past, thrived. If Buddhist meditation is to take root in the West, it will have to find a language, a way of speaking, that is suitable for the Western ear. I have myself found inspiration within the tradition of Western poetry, philosophy, and archetypal psychology. What I have found in poetry, and to a lesser degree philosophy and archetypal psychology, is a way of seeing our world that offers an alternative vision to that of modern 'scientific' materialism. I believe that this poetic way of seeing is the sensibility that we need to bring to the tradition of meditation. I believe that it is the poetic eye that offers us a new way of being in the world that can fulfil the Buddhist vision of awareness, compassion, and a fully human and humane life.

Let's be clear from the beginning: this is not a manual about how to meditate. This is not meditation for 'idiots' or 'dummies'. What I am trying to offer here is an approach to meditation that is a challenge both to the way we experience ourselves and to the way in which we see and 'be' in the world. It is a challenge to transform ourselves.

This to my mind is completely compatible with the ancient tradition of Buddhism. What the historical Buddha offered was not a panacea for the ills of his time, but rather a radical alternative way of living in the world. I believe that this radical alternative way of being in the world is still as valid today as it was 2,500 years ago. At the very heart of this radical vision was the art of meditation. Meditation is then the art of transformation – transforming our innermost impulses of greed, hatred, and delusion into the joy of letting go, love, and wisdom. We might, perhaps, say it is the secret twin of the modern 'god' of progress. For, while progress is all about domination and exploitation of what is outside of us, meditation is all about the coming into relationship with what is inside of us. Although it is a secret twin, far from being the shadow it is the light.

We need to look around the world; we need desperately to take in the kind of world that we are every day creating for ourselves, and for all the other living things that we share this world with. We think of this world as being outside, but in fact it is primarily inside of us. To look about the world means more than anything else to look inside of ourselves. To understand the degradation of the planet means to experience it as an inner loss, a loss of our own 'soul'. This is a poetic, not a religious, way of speaking. I want no truck with God, who has on the whole been part of the problem rather than part of the solution. Meditation is not a religious practice, but neither is it primarily a therapeutic practice. Rather, I think we might call it a 'soulful' practice.

What do I mean by soul?

I have decided to use the language of the soul, and indeed soul is one of the central ideas that I will be using within this book. Some readers may be wondering: why is a Buddhist teacher using this Christian concept, not found in Buddhism? After all, a defining premise of Buddhism is that there is nothing essential to be found in the self, there is no eternal or absolute core that we could call a soul or 'atman'. So, for this concept of a soul to be useful to us, we must be clear that it has little to do with the Christian idea of soul, that is to say, it does not imply anything permanent or independent from the body. We will not here be concerned with the philosophical questions of what happens to us at death, but rather we will be concerned with the idea of soul as it affects us in our lives.

In doing so, I am following the work of archetypal psychologists, in particular the work of James Hillman. (This does not mean that I am slavishly following Hillman – rather that I feel I am within that tradition in which he is one of the major modern figures.) For Hillman, soul is at work in imagination, myth, and metaphor, and soul is contrasted with spirit. Here is one of my favourite Hillman quotes:

> The spiritual point of view always posits itself as superior, and operates particularly well in a fantasy of transcendence among absolutes and ultimates.[1]

History and religion are full of examples of 'spirit' manifesting in the way Hillman characterizes it. Spirit when separated from soul becomes the justification and source of energy for all types of inhumanity. The genocide of the indigenous peoples of North

America, for instance, was rationalized as the 'manifest destiny' of the spiritually superior white Europeans. Hillman highlights the dangers of spirit when it becomes an abstract idea separated from the direct felt experience, which he calls soul. It is our connection with what we are calling soul, which includes an awareness of our own and others' vulnerability, that keeps us from treating others as objects.

Following Hillman we can, perhaps, get a greater sense of soul by contrasting it further with spirit. Spirit has an affinity with fire, its direction is upwards, it is hot and dry. In contrast, soul tends downwards, it is damp or moist. Spirit has an affinity with light and clarity; soul tends towards complexity and is often obscure. Spirit tends to be logical and linear; soul is associative and meandering.

More than anything else, meditation offers a way in which an imbalance between these ideas of spirit and soul can be addressed. This might all sound rather grandiose, yet what is being called for here is not at all grandiose – it is in fact something to do with intimacy and taking care. Meditation asks us to turn towards ourselves with love and care. It is only when we do this that we will then be able to turn towards the world with the same love and care. Here is a poem by Robinson Jeffers that expresses this sentiment wonderfully:

Carmel Point
by Robinson Jeffers

The extraordinary patience of things!
This beautiful place defaced with a crop of suburban
    houses –
How beautiful when we first beheld it,
Unbroken field of poppy and lupin walled with clean cliffs;
No intrusion but two or three horses pasturing,
Or a few milch cows rubbing their flanks on the outcrop
    rockheads –
Now the spoiler has come: does it care?
Not faintly. It has all time. It knows the people are a tide
That swells and in time will ebb, and all

Their works dissolve. Meanwhile the image of the pristine
  beauty
Lives in the very grain of the granite,
Safe as the endless ocean that climbs our cliff. – As for us:
We must uncenter our minds from ourselves;
We must unhumanize our views a little, and become
  confident
As the rock and ocean that we were made from.[2]

It is paradoxically our very self-centredness that stops us turning towards ourselves and turning towards the world. These are some of the things that we will be investigating within this book, but we are not going to find any answers. This book is not about answers. This is not a book offering solutions, remedies, cures, or I hope any other kind of snake oil; rather it is a book that tries to raise the questions that need to be asked, and tries to encourage readers to investigate them themselves.

Meditation is then, more than anything else, a way of investigating our soul. In this sense, soul stands for what is below the surface of us, at the heart of us. It stands for what we tend to turn away from in ourselves. It stands for what we see out of the corner of our eyes. For, unlike spirit, soul is not easy to pin down. Here I am reminded of William Blake's engraving of Isaac Newton measuring the universe with a pair of dividers. The image is trying to remind us that rationality has its limitations, that not everything can be measured and counted. And this is the case with the soul: it cannot be clearly delineated, it cannot be weighed, it cannot even be fully described. Indeed, soul is not really a thing at all, rather a quality, or even a texture or taste. It is a feeling that a person or building or work of art might have. It is, perhaps, what makes us fall quiet when we enter certain buildings or landscapes. It is the quality that certain poems or books have, the ones we come back to again and again.

We can think of soul and spirit as representing two different ways of looking at the world. From the perspective of spirit, soul is very frustrating. It is frustrating because it cannot be pinned down or defined. Much of our spiritual practice is in the thrall of spirit. Whenever we encounter a spiritual teacher who seems to offer us the answers to the questions of life, we have found a teacher who is addressing not the soul but the spirit within us, for the spirit is always on the lookout for the answer, the quick fix, the big breakthrough that will put everything right. This is the spirit's fantasy. In contrast, the last words of the historical Buddha were a heartfelt entreaty to his followers to be a light unto themselves:

> Monks, be islands unto yourselves, be your own refuge, having no other; let the Dhamma be an island and a refuge to you, having no other. Those who are islands unto themselves [...] should investigate to the very heart of things.[3]

The teachings of the Buddha have to be understood individually by each of us, or rather they have to be *experienced* by each of us. There is not some answer out there; rather, there is a way of coming into an intimate relationship with our own psyche, and this is the way of meditation.

I have a painful memory from my early twenties of a good friend of mine who suffered from depression. One time when I went to see her, she was very excited and insisted on showing me some book she had just read. It seemed to me like New Age pap, but she was convinced that it offered her the solution to all her difficulties. I did not have the heart then to try and argue against it; a few months later she killed herself. If we are forever on the lookout for the 'solution' – one day crystal healing, the next past-life regression – we are really not in the place to confront the real nature of ourselves and the world.

Lastly, the idea of soul as it will be used in this book has everything to do with the body. It has everything to do with our lives as we experience them now and therefore with the body, because from the perspective of meditation the body is a metaphor for the psyche. This body is below, and so it is our own underworld. The soul is then another way of speaking of the psyche, and metaphorically the psyche is to be found by paying attention to the body. This is to say that the soul is to be found in paying attention to direct experience.

Within meditation, direct experience is found in the sensations and feelings of the body, in the images and ideas that rise up from the body, as opposed to simply 'ideas'. This is a very important distinction to be made, and it is perhaps best understood through the analogy of dreams. When we dream, we are not making our thoughts up – rather it feels as if our dreams are arising spontaneously. We do not really have dreams – rather they have us, we are in them. When we meditate, we will also have the experience of things seeming to arise independently from the rational mind. I will be referring to the material that arises in this way as 'image'. We need to be clear that the term 'image' does not necessarily imply a visual image. Rather, an image can be a feeling in the body, a sensation, or an emotion, or indeed a thought or visual image – the distinction being that it is not deliberately fabricated by the 'thinking' mind.

In practice, the distinction we are making here is not absolute. In practice, it is not possible to clearly delineate between what we might call the soul arising into consciousness and constructions of our rational mind. Nevertheless, it is important that we bear this distinction in mind, although it might be difficult, in practice, to distinguish between constructed fantasies of a bored mind and the spontaneous presentations of soul. As with so much of what we will encounter as meditators, it will not be possible to pin down the exact nature of our experiences. One of the characteristics of what we are calling soul is, as we have already noted, its ambiguous character. In this regard, meditation is best understood as a poetic experience, just as, when we read a poem, it has many meanings, it reveals itself in different ways at different times, it has no definitive interpretation: we cannot say it means this and nothing else.

I remember going to a reading of the poet Miroslav Holub. I had used one of his poems in a book I had written about meditation (and I will quote him again later in this book), so I took along a copy of my book to give him. As it turned out my publishers had already sent him a copy, and we had a chat about his poem that I had used. Holub, in his rather gruff voice with a heavy Eastern European accent, said, 'The use of my poem was entirely...' Here he seemed to pause, and I found myself fearing that I was going to be told off by one of my poetic heroes, so I was relieved that his next word was 'appropriate'. What he went on to say I found very interesting. He told me that he had written the poem as a response to the political oppression in his native Czechoslovakia, and, while I had used his poem to illustrate something quite different, he said to me that he felt my use of his poem was very appropriate because this was the wonderful thing about poetry: it has no fixed meaning – in essence, good poetry is never literal. It is this non-literal essence of poetry that gives it an affinity with what we are calling soul. So our approach to meditation in this book is what we might call a poetic approach. We might also call it a soulful approach, and this is a way of being in the world, a way of seeing the world, and of responding to ourselves and to the world.

I hope that you are beginning to get a feel for what we will be concerned with in this book. It should be clear that it is not a technical manual about meditation, nor is it a 'spiritual' book offering answers to knotty metaphysical questions. It is not going to tell you, or show you, the way to become 'enlightened'. Indeed, to the extent that we will consider enlightenment at all, we will consider it as a metaphor, as a poetic expression not to be taken literally. I am aware that this will be a disappointment to some readers. Many people take up meditation and other spiritual practices because they like the idea of becoming enlightened. This is an ego fantasy. It is the ultimate materialistic fantasy. We may like to believe that there is a state of being, which we call 'enlightenment', that will put us above all psychological and worldly difficulties. However, I believe very strongly that the purpose of practice is to bring it into the world. In the words of the poet Wallace Stevens, 'the way through the world is more difficult to find than the way beyond it.'[4] This approach might seem to go against traditional Buddhism. As we will see, however, this is to take the teachings of the Buddha in an overliteral way. We will return to this later on, but for now we will leave this rather contentious subject.

Part 1

Grounding

Chapter one

....

Grounding as image

Grounding is in many ways the most central element of this book. The 'image' of grounding is the central image of Buddhism, and it is in this image we seek the foundation for our meditation. My contention is that this image corresponds with what the Buddha taught as the first noble truth, the truth of dukkha, or suffering. The other three noble truths teach us that craving is the source of our suffering, that there is an end to suffering, and that the end is found by following the noble eightfold path. But it is with dukkha or suffering that we have to begin. So here we are concerned with dukkha as it relates to being grounded.

To ground means to come fully into our present experience; it is the means by which we fully realize our present situation. We can see this 'image' of grounding being directly expressed as 'posture'. Through this image, we are seeking to find what is at the heart of our practice. We are going to use this as our touchstone, and so we need to look into our chosen image further.

Grounding has to be 'remembered' as an archetypal image. Firstly, what is meant here by 'image'? Image implies something that we 'see', however the 'seeing' is of a particular type. It is psychological in that it is related to the psyche. This gives us our first impression of grounding. It is related to the psyche and as such to the body. We are grounded in the psyche through attending to the body.

Grounding means to come into an active relationship to the image of grounding. It might seem rather convoluted to talk about grounding primarily as an image, but it is important to understand that everything we experience is image in its broadest sense. This is what the human mind does: it makes image. So whatever we experience we can call image. Without image there is no experience. Another way of talking about this is to say that the human mind is self-reflective: it is aware of what it is aware of, and in order to be reflectively aware it has to make image. It is this type of awareness, self-reflective awareness, that we are interested in as meditators, and as human beings. But for the moment let's leave aside this rather theoretical consideration of the nature of image, and turn towards the image itself as it appears archetypally within the Buddhist tradition.

Even people who know very little about Buddhism will be aware of sculptural representations of the Buddha. These come in many forms, but by far the most ubiquitous is that of the seated Buddha in the meditation posture.

If you look closely, you will see that many of these images show the right hand extended as if the Buddha is tapping the earth with the tips of his fingers. Such statues, or pictures, represent the historical Buddha during his enlightenment. The extended right hand is known as the earth-touching mudrā. A mudrā is a hand gesture with symbolic significance. The significance of this particular mudrā is quite mysterious. According to the mythology of the Buddhist enlightenment, having seated himself under the bodhi tree, the Buddha is challenged by a figure known as Mara, who occupies a somewhat similar position to that of Satan in the story of Christ. Mara appears to the Buddha in order to challenge his right to sit under the bodhi tree, which is the place where all Buddhas are said to have gained enlightenment. At first, Mara and his legions of daemons attack the Buddha with every conceivable type of weapon. The Buddha-to-be remains seated in perfect serenity, and the deadly weapons on touching his aura turn into beautiful flower petals and fall harmlessly around him. Having failed with this assault, Mara then tries to undermine the confidence of the would-be Buddha through the rhetoric of a deceiver, declaring that the would-be Buddha has no witness to testify for him in regards to his right to become enlightened. And it is in answer to this challenge that the Buddha extends his right arm and taps the earth with his fingertips. Here is part of a traditional account of this episode:

The Bodhisattva replied: 'Mara, this earth is my witness.'
And the Bodhisattva enveloped Mara and all his following
with a thought proceeding from love and compassion. He
was like a lion, without distress or fear, terror or weakness,
without dejection, without confusion, without agitation,
without the dread which makes the hair stand on end.

With his right hand [...] he touched all parts of his
body, and then gently touched the earth. And at that
moment he uttered this verse:

This earth, the home of all beings,
is impartial and free of malice
towards everything which moves or does not move.
Here is the guarantee that there is no deception;
Take the earth as my witness,

And as the Bodhisattva touched the great earth, it trembled
in six ways: it trembled, trembled strongly, trembled
strongly on all sides; resounded, resounded strongly,
resounded strongly on all sides. Just as the bronze bells
from Magadha ring out when struck with a stick, so this
great earth resounded and resounded again when touched
by the hand of the Bodhisattva.

Then the goddess of the earth, the goddess named
Sthāvarā, surrounded by a following of a hundred times
ten million earth goddesses, shook the whole great earth.
Not far from the Bodhisattva, she revealed the upper half
of her body adorned with all its ornaments, and bowing
with joined palms, spoke thus to the Bodhisattva:

'Just so, Great Being. It is indeed as you have declared!
We appear here to attest to it. Moreover, O Bhagavat, you
yourself have become the supreme witness of both the
human and the god realms. In truth you are the purest of
all beings.'

Having heard the voice from the earth,
the deceiver and his army, terrified and broken,
began to flee. Like foxes in the wood
who hear the lion's roar,
like crows at the fall of a clump of earth,
all suddenly dispersed.[5]

Clearly, we are not meant to take this story literally.
Buddhism has on the whole avoided the literalism that has
tended to plague the mainstream Judaeo-Christian traditions,
which in my opinion is due mainly to the fact that they are
monotheistic in nature. If we apply my understanding of soul,
paradoxically perhaps, we can say that these traditions lack soul.

When any tradition becomes dominated by spirit, it can
no longer tolerate any sort of uncertainty or ambiguity. The
spiritual perspective demands certainty and clarity, and because
of this the metaphorical or poetic nature of myth is lost, and we
find ourselves in the ridiculous situation where we are asked to
take stories such as that of the biblical flood to be literally true.
Paradoxically this tendency towards literalism is connected to
the overvaluing of the rationalistic aspect of the human psyche. I
realize that it is very unfashionable to talk negatively about other
religions; however, I feel it is important to try to be as truthful
as one is able. It is my opinion that monotheistic religions do
a great disservice to the human psyche, at least when they are
held onto in a dogmatic and literal way. It might well be true,
for example, as thinkers following the ideas of the nineteenth-

century sociologist Max Weber have argued, that the Protestant interpretation of Christianity is conducive to capitalism and thus has instilled in us a strong work ethic. However, I am not an uncritical fan of capitalism: under its banner we are making a fetish of progress and growth that is both unfortunate in its consequences for the world and unsustainable.

From the perspective of our image of grounding, both monotheism and consumerism in its present rampant form are profoundly unhelpful. As we saw in our story about the Buddha gaining enlightenment when he touched the ground, the earth goddess is accompanied by a countless number of other goddesses. Here we get a sense of the polytheistic sympathies of Buddhism; Buddhism is a secular belief to the extent that it does not hold it helpful to believe in a creator god. Nevertheless, imaginatively for the traditional Buddhist, the world is full of gods and goddesses and many other types of non-human sentient beings. In contrast, monotheism moves to eradicate all other supernatural agencies: it is often unable to tolerate anything that is not under its own direct power – all such other forces become evil. The consequence of this for the psychology of the believer is that any aspect of character or personality that does not conform to this narrow understanding is unacknowledged and becomes suppressed. In the worst case, this leads to fanaticism that has no empathy with the other. Historically this intolerance has been directed against all sorts of schisms, as well as pagan witches, other monotheistic faiths, and so on. Monotheism tends towards intolerance, and from a psychological point of view it often results in repression and is therefore not conducive to developing a sense of intimacy with our own innately polytheistic psyche.

Monotheism places power above: the god of monotheism is always the sky god, imaginatively above, looking down. Therefore in order to be in touch with God there has to be a going up, a reaching towards heaven, and as we have seen it is the spirit which moves upwards, while the soul tends downwards towards earth. Of course there is a place for sky gods within the imagination and therefore the spirit, but they need to be balanced by earth gods and goddesses as well as underworld deities. It is no coincidence that the psychology of Sigmund Freud sees the conscious ego in a struggle against an unconscious id. This view in many ways mirrors the monotheistic religious background from which Freud came. A psychology that advocates the dominance of the ego over a chaotic and dangerous id mirrors God's battle against the forces of evil. Both monotheism and the psychology that sprang from it work against coming into a relationship of care towards the soul.

As for consumerism, when it becomes the main motivating factor within our lives, it puts us in a state of constant anxiety, where we are looking for a sense of worth outside of ourselves. This is a profoundly ungrounding state of being, characterized by restlessness and superficiality. It is not unreasonable to say that consumerism has become the new religion. In contrast, in the Buddhist tradition we see that the idea of 'going forth', which traditionally meant giving up the worldly life for a life of simplicity, was a prerequisite for leading the Buddhist life. Of course we do not have to take this idea of going forth too literally. It does, however, suggest a particular attitude that is oriented towards finding a sense of value in non-materialistic aspects of our lives.

There is also a more sinister aspect underlying the modern cult of consumerism, which makes fully facing up to a situation – what we will be calling 'turning towards' – very difficult and painful. This aspect is the knowledge, albeit hidden, that we are collectively responsible for the violation of the natural world. Our inability to turn towards is partly due to a reluctance to face up to the real situation in which we find ourselves, for turning towards will necessitate us experiencing the grief and sense of loss that are inherent in our turning away from the earth. For such a turning away is a turning away from our essential self or, at least, a very important aspect of our essential self.

In addition, consumerism reinforces the seeing of the world as what Heidegger would term a 'standing resource': the eye of consumerism reveals the world as other and as an object to be used. The natural world is increasingly preserved, as if it were an ancient object, in nature preserves, areas of natural beauty, national parks, and so on, where we go to view the world as if it were something exotic and other. Having preserved specimens of the natural world, we are free to exploit the 'real' world free of guilt.

But perhaps the most pernicious aspect of modern life is simply its obsessive busyness. This seems to me, even in my lifetime, to have become exponentially worse. Multitasking has become not a useful skill to be used in exceptional circumstances but rather the norm, even when it is completely unnecessary. Many people now seem unable to give their full attention to others, and are instead constantly checking their phones or some other electronic device. It seems that a neurotic compulsion to be connected is becoming increasingly common. However, the nature of the connection is often superficial and pushes the possibility of deep intimacy into the shadows.

It now seems impossible for many people to do nothing, yet doing nothing is a vital part of our lives. To be constantly busy, to have constant external input, keeps us in a state of frantic mental activity. This is now so common as to go unnoticed until it becomes chronic and causes mental or physical illness. Perhaps the most important and fundamental thing we are doing when we try to meditate is simply reducing the amount of mental activity. Although I am guilty, as are many others, of writing books about meditation, in essence meditation is very simple. It is just doing nothing or at least less. Indeed, one of the most valuable things about meditation is that it allows us to realize just how overactive our mind is. The source of the overactivity I am talking about here is quite different from the conscious application of the mind to a creative or valuable task. When the mind is fully engaged in a creative activity, the feeling we have is one of absorption and often pleasure. This is quite different from distracting ourselves. I am not suggesting that we should all sit around doing nothing all the time. However, an inability to do nothing and just be is one of the major symptoms of a life out of balance. This is particularly true in relation to mental activity. My own teacher once remarked, 'Too much thinking is pathological.' We need to be able to allow the mind to relax, and meditation is one way to begin to get a sense of what it might feel like to have a mind that is not habitually frantic – though in and of itself this is not enough.

What meditation provides is a window onto a new way of being in the world, rather than a panacea for all our mental distress. If we meditate but do nothing else to help this slowing down of the mind, it is unrealistic to expect any dramatic improvement. What meditation can do is act as a catalyst for change: it can be the beginning of change in our lives, of gaining the confidence that we need to begin to reconstruct our lives so they are lived in harmony both with our deeper selves and with the world. I think it is important that we do not have exaggerated expectations of what meditation will do for us. We should be on guard when people offer revolutionary or radical techniques requiring little effort that claim to solve all of our problems. This is the naive fantasy unfortunately peddled by many self-styled gurus or spiritual teachers. There is no technique out there, no secret method, no holy man or woman with a spiritual magic wand. Spirituality has become part of the consumerist culture of our age, but in reality it is not something we can buy off the peg.

Okay, enough of the cautionary warning. Let us turn to the actual topic of grounding itself. The first thing to say is that our present idea of what it means to be grounded may not necessarily be very accurate. Grounding has become one of the terms of the New Age, and often when people hear it they think it means a comfortable relaxed state where they are free of anxiety and worry. Of course this is, broadly speaking, the kind of state that we are looking for in the long run. However, when viewed as a process, grounding may require us, and very probably will require us, to go through a certain amount of anxiety and emotional and physical discomfort. Grounding in the sense in which I mean it here is a radical challenge to our habitual state of being. It is therefore to be expected that it will be resisted by our ego.

Chapter two

....

Beginning to ground: the role of a good posture

Perhaps the first thing that we have to do is to find a way of sitting that works for us. I have stressed that the central motif of this book is the image of the Buddha in meditation; however, most of us will not be able to sit, physically, like the Buddha. What is important is not so much achieving some kind of yogic perfection, but rather the attitude or spirit that we bring to our sitting. The qualities that we bring to posture are the same qualities that we try to bring to all aspects of meditation practice. This gives us an important clue: the posture is not something that we do as a preparation for meditation – it is the meditation.

The qualities we will be emphasizing throughout this book are the qualities of kindness and awareness, and these are the very same qualities that we need to bring to finding our way of sitting. There is no single 'right' posture: what is right for you is going to depend on your age, flexibility, and so on. For some people with back problems, for example, their best option might be to lie down in a posture such as the one recommended by the Alexander technique. For others, a chair might be their best option. Whatever our posture, we are trying to allow the spine to be reasonably upright. More important, though, than the physical aspects of posture, or perhaps I should say integral to the physical aspects of posture, is attitude. In the past, the word 'attitude' was used to describe one's physical posture as well as one's mental characteristics, so we can think of attitude as relating to both our physical posture and our mental approach to that posture.

And, although it might sound strange, posture is also about the cultivation of an image, by which I mean there is an inner – we can even say secret – posture. This inner or secret posture is related to the image that we have of ourselves as meditators. What I am trying to convey, by referring to a secret posture, is that the posture is not primarily physical, or rather our normal idea of physicality is very limited and does not include the very many subtle aspects of body that are integral to good posture. Fortunately – or unfortunately, I am not sure – the more subtle aspects of posture cannot really be taught. They have to be experienced by the individual, and even when experienced by the individual they cannot really be made into a technique. It is more that we learn to trust and get on with the body. There is something fundamental and important in this: we are not trying to impose good posture on the body, rather we are trying to learn from the body, from our own bodies. We might use the metaphor of listening – listening to what our bodies are telling us about how they wish to sit. However, this is not an easy thing to do, and it will probably take us many years of practice to really tune in to the subtle energies of our bodies and to move from imposing an idea of posture upon the body to listening to this secret image of posture that comes from the body itself.

I realize that this is not an easy way of talking about posture, for it lacks any real precision. However, I am trying to suggest that within our body is an innate image that can be allowed to express itself if and when we are able to get out of the way. So much of what we are going to be looking at comes down to this getting out of the way. What we want to get out of the way of is what we might refer to as our ego. This term 'ego' is not completely satisfactory, so maybe it is worth exploring what it might mean in relation to posture.

It is very common in classes to see people sitting in a way that is not conducive to trying to cultivate kind awareness. You can often see that they are forcing themselves into a posture that is putting a strain on their bodies. When people do this, they usually become very uncomfortable and fidgety within a short time. However, quite often when you point this out to them they say something like, 'Oh no, it's fine – I like to sit like this.' They have an idea that they should be sitting cross-legged, and, even though they are very uncomfortable, they are not prepared to give up their idea. It is the ego at work: they think that if they cannot sit like the teachers they are not doing it right, or they are not as good as the teacher – they are not a good meditator. Whenever we get into thinking we are not a good meditator, we are to some extent or other involved with ego. We cannot avoid this; to think that we can is also ego, so we begin to see that ego is a very difficult thing, it is a very slippery fish, and whenever we think we have caught it, it will slip from our grasp. But we do not have to worry about catching it, even less defeating it.

Ego is not something that we need to defeat, it is not something that we need to destroy: this too is an ego fantasy. In fact it is one of the main fantasies that occurs within the spiritual life. It is a bit like St George and the dragon. It is often pointed out that the destruction of the dragon tends to be found within the Western interpretations of this myth, while in the Eastern equivalent of the myth the dragon is not destroyed but rather befriended. While the ego is very slippery and cunning, it is also rather fragile: it is very easily hurt, and what we don't want is a hurt ego, as that really is a nuisance. When we begin to understand our practice as an investigation into ourselves, an act of research, which is to look again and again, we understand that what we need to do is to see what the ego is up to. If our intention is to catch it or destroy it, it will become very tricky and will hide from us, become increasingly devious, but if our attitude is one of kind enquiry then it will show itself to us and, when we see it, it is not really a problem at all – it is just there doing what it does, and we can acknowledge it and get on with what we are doing.

I am sorry about this digression – well of course I am not really: digression is one of the characteristics of soul, so no doubt we will have many more. And there is something in this that is relevant to our subject. For if we have the idea that meditation is going to be straightforward without deviation, we are going to be disappointed.

So broadly speaking, there are four ways we may sit, or rather three, plus the option of lying down.

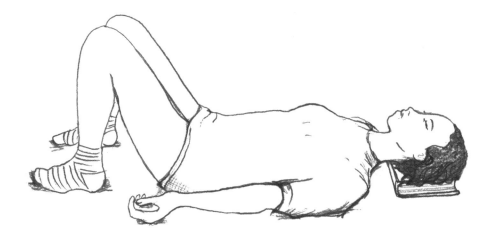

Let us deal with lying down first, for, even if we do not use this posture for formal meditation, we will be using it for various relaxation exercises. I have taken this way of lying down from the Alexander technique. In my mind, it has the advantage over the yoga corpse posture of being more conducive to staying awake. In the Alexander semi-supine position, we have the back of our head resting on a hard surface, something like a book. You can calculate the thickness of the book to use by standing in a naturally upright position with your back to the wall, the heels of your feet touching the wall. Get a friend to measure the distance between the back of your head and the wall: this is the thickness of the book you need to rest your head upon. The head should be placed on the book in such a way that the neck is free. That means it is the base of the skull that is resting on the book. So you are lying on your back with your head resting on the book, but the soles of your feet flat on the floor so your knees are in the air. Your legs being like this is an important part of the posture: it means that when you start to fall asleep your knees will tend to fall apart or together, either way alerting you to the fact that you are falling asleep. It also has the advantage of helping the lower back to relax, and to allow letting go in the big muscles of the upper legs and buttocks. Your hands can be by your side or resting on your lower belly, whichever feels most comfortable for you. It can be quite nice to have the hands placed on the belly, as it makes us more aware of our breath. Though it is some years since I had any Alexander lessons myself, I am a big fan of this particular posture, and it is a good alternative for those who cannot sit in a more conventional upright position.

In the Alexander technique, we are often told to imagine 'directions', so, for instance, we might be instructed to imagine the back of a head moving towards the wall behind it while also imagining the base of our spine moving towards the opposite wall. In addition, we might imagine our shoulders moving apart, allowing the back and chest to broaden. What Frederick Matthias Alexander discovered is that our ideas have a profound effect on our physicality. This is a vital insight when it comes to posture and indeed meditation in general. It points to the crucial interpenetration of mind and body; indeed this dualistic way of talking – body and mind – is really quite misleading. It is so entrenched in the Western philosophical tradition, however, that it is very hard to avoid. Of course, it has its uses, and as long as we do not take it literally it is not too bad. But there does seem to be, in the Western tradition, a real tendency to think that the mind is somehow independent and distinct from the body.

This can perhaps be traced back to the Christian idea of soul, which as I have pointed out is quite different from the way we are using the term. In the Christian tradition, the soul is somehow capable of an independent existence from the body, which is seen as a temporary house for the soul. I think it is fair to say that in the European Enlightenment the central idea of the Christian soul was replaced by the idea of rationality, which like the soul it replaced was somehow understood as having an independent existence from the body. While nobody believed this literally, rationality was placed above physicality – this was all part of the European Enlightenment movement of man to centre stage. It was rationality that separated man from the rest of creation. Often this rationality was not extended to women or so-called primitive people, and the white European male reigned supreme on account of this rationality and intellect.

If we bring this prejudice to meditation, we tend to want to ignore the body, seeing it as animal or primitive, and as having nothing to do with the spiritual. At best, posture then becomes something we have to sort out in order to get on with the real stuff of meditation, which is all about the mind. I think this is the single greatest prejudice that we need to overcome if we are going to have an effective meditation practice. This does not mean that our abilities to think creatively and clearly are not extremely important aspects of meditation – they are. However, we often confuse this ability to think in a creative way with the obsessive activity of overstimulated brains. More seriously still, we look for a sense of identity in this frantic thinking. One of the main things that we are trying to do through meditation is to disidentify with this constant static.

As I have already mentioned, and will no doubt mention again, we are much better thinking of meditation as something to do with the body. This is not the body as opposed to the mind, because there is no body as opposed to the mind, or rather there is no mind as opposed to the body. It is rather cumbersome to always have to refer to the mind–body complex, so in this book, whenever I talk about body, I am not talking about it in contrast to, or in opposition to, mind, or if I do so I will make it clear I am doing so. Body does not exclude the mind, and mind has no independent reality outside of the body.

So to return to posture: all of us should practise lying down. These days, when I start a retreat, for the first couple of days I get people to do a lot of lying down.

From a meditation point of view, nothing really interesting will happen until we have started to relax a little. Some people like to 'just get on with it', but this approach so typical of our culture, where there is never enough time, is not usually very useful. We should never approach meditation with the attitude that we do not have enough time, but particularly on retreat the first thing that we need to do is *relax*.

The Myth of Meditation

Keeping quiet
by Pablo Neruda

Now we will count to twelve
and we will all keep still
for once on the face of the earth,
let's not speak in any language;
let's stop for a second,
and not move our arms so much.
It would be an exotic moment
without rush, without engines;
we would all be together
in a sudden strangeness.
Fishermen in the cold sea
would not harm whales
and the man gathering salt
would not look at his hurt hands.
Those who prepare green wars,
wars with gas, wars with fire,
victories with no survivors,
would put on clean clothes
and walk about with their brothers
in the shade, doing nothing.
What I want should not be confused
with total inactivity.
Life is what it is about...
If we were not so single-minded
about keeping our lives moving,
and for once could do nothing,
perhaps a huge silence
might interrupt this sadness
of never understanding ourselves
and of threatening ourselves with
death.
Now I'll count up to twelve
and you keep quiet and I will go.[6]

Lastly, here are the other three ways to sit that I mentioned earlier.

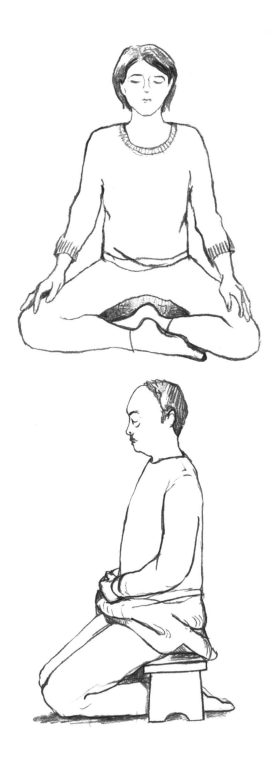

The Myth of Meditation

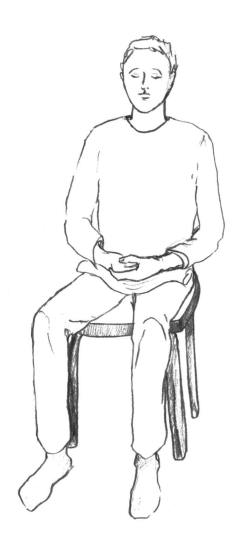

Chapter three

....

Trusting what is there

The first practical exercises in this book will be done lying down, and will be oriented towards letting go and beginning to learn to trust the earth that supports us. In addition, when lying down in the way I have described above, our head is aligned and our back is in the right position, which helps us get a sense of the alignment we are looking for when we sit in an upright position. When we lie down in this manner, we should try and be conscious of what it feels like; in particular, we should pay attention to the relationship of the head to the pelvis, imagining the spine joining the skull to the pelvis. We often tend to think that the spine ends at the base of the neck, but of course it goes right up into our brain stem.

Let's do a simple lying-down exercise. Before we do so, I just want to say a little about all the exercises and meditations that you will find in this book. They are not to be taken as technical instructions – they should be understood as suggestive rather than directive. They do not need to be followed slavishly, so you should try and get a feel for what is being pointed towards and adapt the instructions as suits you. I hope that is clear, because this is the way in which we need to approach meditation in general: we need to be open to what actually happens, what things actually feel like to us, and to allow our own intuition and imagination to play a part.

 Lying down and letting the earth support us

Lying in the semi-supine position, take a few slightly deeper breaths than normal, breathing in through the nose and out through the mouth. Notice the movement in the abdomen, and notice the feeling of the back against the floor. Letting the breathing return to normal, just lie there breathing for a while.

Begin to notice the parts of the body that are in direct contact with the floor, including the soles of the feet (it is probably best if the feet are bare). Notice that you can feel your breath in your body, particularly in the back of the body, which is in contact with the ground beneath it. Regardless of where you are meditating, have a sense that the floor you are lying on is connected down into the earth, through the structure of the building in which you are lying (if you can do this outside in your garden or in a field, that is great); try to have a sense that you are being supported by the earth, that your body is breathing against the earth.

Notice what it feels like to have nothing to do, to have stopped, at least physically, to have stopped moving about. Notice whether this makes you feel calm or anxious; don't try and change it – just notice. We are trying to imagine the earth below us, supporting us. Do this in quite a light sort of way: don't try and force anything – it is a light imagining, perhaps even playful. Be aware of your breath and therefore your body; be aware that your body is supported on the ground. Try and imagine just giving your body to gravity. Notice the kind of thoughts and feelings, the emotions and perhaps images that arise as you lie there. Try not to drift off; if necessary keep coming back, in a calm way, to the breath, to your breath. Keep feeling the weight of your body resting against the earth. Do this for about 10 minutes, or longer if it feels appropriate.

So this is our first exercise: it is very simple and you cannot do it wrong. There is nothing in particular that is meant to happen, rather we are just interested in what does happen. This is going to be a constant refrain throughout this book: just being interested in what our experience is. No doubt you will sometimes get caught up with your thoughts, maybe start fantasizing, or maybe start feeling uncomfortable and fidgeting around a little. You should expect all these things to happen and not worry too much about them. When they happen, we do our best to notice them; sometimes we will be successful and often we will not – this is okay, it is just how it is for us. We are just interested in how it is to lie on the floor, with nothing much to do, being aware of our breath when we remember to, and perhaps having a sense of the earth supporting our body as we lie there breathing.

In this simple exercise, we have the beginnings of meditation – not the beginnings in the sense that we are going to move on to something far more profound, but the beginnings in that slowly, over time, we will be deepening our ability to stay with our experience. I have been meditating for thirty years now, and when I first started to meditate I wanted to experience all sorts of wonderful spiritual states. Now when I meditate I am interested in what is happening. This is a very hard thing for people to really take on: it takes a kind of confidence, just to be with what is going on in a simple, non-judgemental kind way. This point needs to be made as clearly as possible: taking an interest in our actual experience, rather than striving for some idea we have about what our experience should be, is the basis of genuine meditation.

This can be understood in reference to the basic teachings of Buddhism. According to the teachings of the Buddha, our suffering is caused by constant craving for things to be different from what they really are. This craving takes two basic forms: it expresses itself on the one hand as grasping and on the other as aversion – these are two sides of the same coin. When we experience something pleasurable, we wish to have more of it and try to hold onto it: this is what Buddhism means by grasping. By contrast, when we experience something unpleasant, we wish it to go away, we want it to end: this is what Buddhism means by aversion. Sometimes we experience this craving in a very obvious way. However, this craving goes on more or less all the time, often on a very subtle level so that we have no awareness of it at all.

One of the ways of looking at meditation is that we are trying to become more sensitive to and aware of the subtle ways in which craving affects our lives. When we want something to happen in meditation, usually a more pleasurable or interesting state of mind, we are in the grip of some form of craving. This does not mean that we are not interested in cultivating calm, kind, and aware states of mind; rather it means that we recognize that the way to move towards such states of mind is to engage with our experience as it is, as opposed to trying to cover it up with a kind of positive gloss. This is why Buddhism begins with the notion of suffering: it is only when we come into relationship with our suffering that we are in a position to begin to deal with it. The Buddha is often said to have expressed his basic teaching of the four noble truths outlined earlier following the ancient medical formulation of illness, cause, possibility of cure, and remedy. So, when we do not fully acknowledge our basic experience, we are in the position of the patient who refuses to believe that they are ill. While it is relatively easy to know when we are physically ill, it can be a lot harder to recognize suffering when it is of the soul. Indeed, many of the problems that we have – stress, anxiety, that feeling of not belonging – are denied by us unless they become so chronic that we have to address them. Through meditation, we can become more sensitive and aware of how our mind really is, and this is the first vital step towards being able to do something about it.

Unfortunately, it is not enough just to know that we are suffering on the intellectual level: we have to know it on a much deeper level, on the level of full experience. This kind of knowing I will be referring to as 'embodied' knowledge. For something to become embodied, it has to be experienced repeatedly, and reflected upon. It is a little like learning to drive: the body has to learn to drive – it is not enough to have an intellectual understanding of how to drive. As I say, unfortunately it is also not enough to have an intellectual understanding that you suffer: it has to be felt, and for most of us it has to be felt in the bones. We all have various strategies and schemes that we believe, at least to some extent, will provide a way of avoiding suffering; we might think that if we got a different job or a new partner or even a new set of smart clothes we would no longer suffer. Of course, part of us knows that these strategies are unlikely to work, nevertheless our tendency towards self-delusion tends to be very strong, and it is only when we begin to see through our plans and strategies that we can make a start on coming into a more creative relationship with the fact that we do suffer. Here is a poem by William Carlos Williams that comes to mind in this respect:

Thursday
by William Carlos Williams

I have had my dream – like others –
and it has come to nothing, so that
I remain now carelessly
with feet planted on the ground
and look up at the sky –
feeling my clothes about me,
the weight of my body in my shoes,
the rim of my hat, air passing in and out
at my nose – and decide to dream no more.[7]

I love this simple poem. It may at first sight seem rather pessimistic, but I do not read it like that. The word 'carelessly' is pivotal, if ambiguous. We can read it as meaning a lack of care or free from cares. It seems to me that Williams is evoking the state of mindfulness, even though I don't think Williams had anything to do with Buddhism or meditation. Nevertheless, it is a perfect description of being in a mindful state, of being in the present moment. Anyone who has been in that state, and we all have from time to time, will know that it is a state free from anxiety and from our usual constant craving to be, or have, something else.

We are taking our time here to find our way back to the topic of grounding. However, what we have been talking about is to my mind very important in relation to our topic. We are trying to become grounded both in the present moment, based on direct felt experience, and, perhaps a little more difficult to understand, in suffering. That is to say that our grounding is in suffering. This sounds a little off-putting, I know, but I do not mean we have to just suffer – rather, I mean we must be willing to be aware of our actual experience, which most of the time will have an element of unsatisfactoriness to it.

It seems a little paradoxical, but when we come into relationship with our suffering, though it does not disappear, it does change in a positive way. When we do this repeatedly, we slowly begin to experience that it is our constant turning away from things as they really are that is so painful. For me, I can read this in the insight in William Carlos Williams' poem. It is not that we have to give up all our dreams, as to have a positive aspiration is clearly important to us; it is more that we have to give up the kind of dreaming that stops us being fully in our lives. When Martin Luther King Jr declared that he had a dream, this was not a turning away, for his dream was based on a full engagement with the suffering of his own people. And this engagement, I suspect, came from a willingness to feel his own suffering, a suffering that gave him empathy with others and meant he himself was an example of a man with what we might call a great soul.

There is something critical about learning to fully relax, in a physical sense, if you want to become grounded in the manner we are talking about here. There is a relationship between muscular tension and mental holding on. By which I mean that psychological turning away from the difficulties of our lives results in the gradual building up of muscular tension within our bodies. Here is a simple exercise that we can use to help us to relax.

 ## Using the breath to release tension in the body

Lie in the same manner as for the previous exercise, in the semi-supine position, and make sure that you are comfortable and warm enough. Take your time just to come to your natural breath, experiencing it as fully as possible. You might like to take a few slightly deeper breaths in through your nose and out through the mouth to begin with. Spend a few minutes just experiencing your body in relationship to the floor that is supporting you, while staying aware of your breath. Feel the back of your body breathing against the floor.

When you feel ready, take your attention down to your feet and imagine that you are breathing in through your feet along with your normal breath. So you are imagining a kind of subtle breath being drawn in through your feet as you breathe in, then as you breathe out imagine that subtle breath breathing out through your feet. You might begin with just the big toes. Take it slowly: as you breathe in, bring your full attention into your feet, then, as you breathe out, imagine just relaxing any tension that you can feel, and imagine this tension draining away into the earth beneath you.

Slowly explore your feet, supported by being aware of your natural breath. You might want to do one foot first, or both together; there are no hard and fast rules – see what feels natural for you. But really try and notice all the small sensations that make up your experience of your feet. While this is a little hard to explain, what we are trying to do is to feel the feet from the inside as it were, rather than have an idea about what the feet feel like. It is as if the 'mind' is in the feet, rather than the brain being aware of them. Notice all the toes, notice where they join the main body of your feet, notice the sole, notice the ball, the instep, the sides of the feet, and so on. This time we're just going to do the feet and nothing else. Take at least 15–20 minutes to do this, so it is a very detailed exploration of your feet. It is very likely that your mind will drift off now and then; don't worry about this, and just come back to the feet whenever you notice you have drifted. The key is really trying to keep a relationship between your natural breathing and the awareness in your feet. When we manage to relax our feet, this will have a sympathetic effect on the whole of our body.

This exercise, like the first, is very simple. It might be that it feels quite a boring thing to do, so perhaps this is a good point to say a little bit about boredom as it relates to meditation. When we spend most of our time in a chronic state of overstimulation, as most of us do these days, boredom becomes very prevalent in our experience. We are unable to concentrate, unable to become absorbed. It is a little bit like people who bolt down their food: they eat a lot but don't tend to taste any of it. Food is not interesting to people who do not taste it. When I am leading a retreat, I use a lot of poetry, all of which I learn by heart. I started to do that because of my failing eyesight, which meant it became increasingly difficult in low-light situations such as meditation halls for me to read. But, while I started to do this out of necessity, it has become a real joy for me. It is quite common for people to say to me, 'I never liked poetry, I found it really boring, but I have really appreciated the poems you used on the retreat', or something similar. I think there are two reasons why poetry in this context can have a very powerful effect on people.

Firstly, they are in a particularly receptive state, where at least some of the normal mental chatter has died away. Secondly, because I have taken time to learn the poems by heart, they are heartfelt, or we could say embodied, and people are sensitive to this, picking up on the intimate relationship I have with the words I speak.

When we engage with something in a superficial way, it is normally boring; it is only when we give ourselves fully to something that it becomes interesting. This ability to give ourselves fully to something, to become absorbed in something, is largely determined by our own state of mind rather than the object of our attention. When we are in a mindful state of mind, a calm state of mind, something very simple like a field daisy reveals its innate beauty and wonder to us. That beauty is there all the time, of course: it is not the daisy that has changed but our way of looking at it.

The only answer there is to boredom is to pay closer attention, to give yourself more fully to what it is you are experiencing at the time. The breath is a great example of this: it is very common for people to say being aware of the breath seems boring to them, but it is only when you give yourself to the breath that it reveals its depth and endless fascinating qualities to you. When we try to be aware of something from the perspective of the grasping ego, we are nearly always quickly bored. This is because the ego is not really interested in anything outside of itself. One of its main defensive mechanisms is boredom. When it is asked to be aware of the feet, for example, it quickly becomes bored. This is because, from the perspective of the ego, the feet are a threat to its own sense of centrality and permanence, which it is desperate to preserve. However, it is possible to be with the feet not from the narrow perspective of the ego, but from the perspective of the feet themselves. Of course, this is just a way of talking – the feet do not really have their own perspective, but they do have a more or less endless succession of sensation as well as emotions, feelings, and even images that arise in association with those sensations. When we look at our language, we begin to see just how symbolic and rich the body is: it is the source of many metaphors; for instance, in the case of the feet, metaphors such as 'feet of clay' or 'to put our best foot forward' readily spring to mind.

Our interest in the body is for the sake of the body itself but also, and perhaps even more importantly, because of the importance of the body in relation to the psyche. We could say we have both a physical body and a psychic body, both the literal body and a metaphorical body, both the body of sensation and a body of emotion. When we relax the body, we are doing much more than just relaxing the body: we are also coming into relationship with our psyche in a different way. When we are out of touch with our body, or have a purely instrumental relationship with our body, we are to some degree cut off from our psyche, from imagination. Although I do not want you to take it literally, I think it is useful to imagine that the psyche is not something that resides within the darkness of the brain but rather something that inhabits the whole of our bodies. We could say we have embodied psyche, and this is why so many of our metaphors that we use to describe experiences of the psyche are metaphors employing different parts of our own bodies: we are hard-hearted or soft-hearted; we lose heart or take heart; we have broken hearts, overflowing hearts, tender hearts; we lose our hearts or give them away. Clearly the heart has more than its fair share of metaphors, but there is hardly a single part of the body that does not have some, that is not involved with the imagination. This is because we know the world primarily through our bodies.

This relationship between the psyche and the body is deeply embedded in the Western tradition, particularly in myth. In Ovid's *Metamorphoses*, for instance, the transformation of the psyche is symbolized through various physical transformations, such as that of Narcissus: the consequence of self-obsession is expressed by the transformation of the beautiful youth into the flower that now bears his name. We can also see this intimate interpenetration of the body and the psyche in the portrayal of characters in the work of many writers, such as Dickens, where characters like Scrooge physically personify their personality, and we also find it strongly present in the history of medicine, in such ideas as the 'four humours'.

Chapter four

. . . .

Remembering the world

Grounding is the first stage in beginning to move away from a perspective dominated by the ego sense. The first thing that we have to do is to put the ego within a context. By this I mean we have to remember that our ego does not exist as an independent entity: it exists only as something created by our own minds. Whenever we meditate, we do so in this context, and simply by remembering this context we begin to have an effect on the dominance of our ego. This next exercise suggests some simple ways in which we can remember the context in which we meditate.

 Meditating in the world

Take up your meditation posture. Spend as much time as you need to make sure that you are as comfortable as possible. Check that your body is aligned – your nose vertically aligned with your navel, your shoulders above your hips, and your ears above the shoulders – and imagine that you are gently pushed in the back of your head up towards the ceiling.

Then just come to your natural breath; feel the parts of your body that are in contact with your cushion and the floor. We are establishing a sense of contact between our bodies and the floor underneath us. Begin to imagine the floor spreading out from the point of contact into the room, and then from the room into the world outside, so you have the sense of sitting in the room and you have the sense that this room is in a building and that the building is in a city or town, or in the countryside. Also imagine that the ground below you goes down, and that you are supported by the deep earth.

We are remembering the world. Listen to the sounds around you; whether they are the sounds of birds singing or the sounds of traffic, notice how these sounds naturally arise in your consciousness. Do not strain to hear

them: just be aware that they are there helping you to be present. Try sitting
for about 20 minutes, just being as present as you can to the world around
you. When you notice that your attention is becoming introverted, that is
you are becoming caught up in some fantasy, remember your breath, your
body, and the world. Our bodies are part of the world, so there is no conflict
between being aware of your body and being aware of the world. I find
sound particularly useful as a support to staying present, so you might put
an emphasis on a relaxed listening to all the sounds around you as well as the
sounds of your own breath.

This exercise is shifting the weight of awareness from our
own internal voice to the voice of the world. It is a simple
beginning in the practice of being aware that we exist by the
grace of the world.

It is a very common misunderstanding that meditation is
all about going inside, shutting out the world, but this is not
the case. We do not exist independently and separately from
the world: we are simply one of the multitudinous ways in
which the world happens to be manifesting. Here is the Miroslav
Holub poem that I mentioned earlier, which I used to open the
first book I wrote about meditation:

The door
by Miroslav Holub

[...]
Go and open the door.
Maybe a dog's rummaging.
Maybe you'll see a face,
or an eye
or the picture
of a picture.
[...]
Go and open the door.
Even if there's only
the darkness ticking
even if there's only
the hollow wind

even if
nothing
is there
go and open the door.
At least
there'll be
a draught.[8]

Meditation is related to being in the world – it has something to do with the sense of being in the world. If you remember our image for grounding, the image of the Buddha-to-be sitting under the bodhi tree and, extending his right hand, tapping the earth with the tips of his fingers to bring forth the earth goddess, we see that Buddhism was concerned with the earth from its very beginning. Its concern for the earth is not on a material level, however, or at least not only on a material one: it is also concerned with the imaginative relationship we have with the earth. It recognizes through this myth that the earth is also part of the human psyche. As such, the earth is important not only because it provides all our material needs, but also in a psychic, or psychological, sense.

We tend to think of meditation as a means of working with our internal 'mind', but on a deeper level meditation is also about coming into a new relationship with the world. This is not the world purely as a material 'thing', rather it is the world as a world soul or *anima mundi*, an idea we can trace back to Plato and no doubt was in existence long before him – indeed it would have come into existence with the human imagination. Even in our scientific age, this idea has found a way into the popular imagination through the Gaia theory of James Lovelock, and something similar is found in nearly all spiritual traditions. It does not matter whether it is literally true, or rather such an insistence on the materialistic idea of truth is just not relevant: it is the truth of the human imagination, in the same way that love is. We might like to dismiss the history of human spirituality as mere superstition, but with such a dismissal we also banish a part of our own selves. When we no longer think of the world as animated, as having a soul, we condemn ourselves to living in a dead world; our obsession with factual truth as the only kind of truth leaves us in danger or finding ourselves without hope or compassion for the world around us.

The German philosopher Heidegger, while perhaps rightly criticized for his political views, nevertheless had a great insight when he understood that revealing the world from the viewpoint of scientific materialistic paradigms necessarily casts a shadow that obscures another part of the world, and in doing so gravely impoverishes the human imagination. This is not to say anything about the objective truth of science or the technologies that flow from it, but to uncover the values that underlie the cult of science and technology that dominates the modern world. Science and technology can often reveal the world as a 'standing resource', which strips the world of its soul. Increasingly, we are beginning to realize that treating the world in this way is unsustainable, that the planet we live on is a delicate natural system that cannot be continuously and casually exploited without dire consequences for us.

While these ecological considerations are of great importance, they are not primarily what concerns us here. Rather, here we are concerned with the corresponding effect that this dominant attitude towards the world has on our minds or souls. Our contention here is that such an attitude reduces us to the level of resource, just as we reduce the world. When I was young, companies had 'personnel departments'; now they have 'human resource departments' – perhaps in this change of terminology is defined a fundamental change in our attitude towards ourselves. This attitude is so pernicious that we hardly question it, yet nevertheless it is a change that has happened relatively recently. With the introduction of mass production, which replaced the idea of craft, the human worker began to be seen as an appendage to the machine, often nothing more than a machine minder. We do not have space here to analyze this in any detail. The point I want to make, however, is that our present values and attitudes are not inevitable: they have replaced other ways of understanding man's relationship to the world. Even a cursory examination of the way so-called primitive people understand the world reveals that there are radical alternatives to the way we understand the world. On an individual level, at least, it is still possible to shift our understanding of the world to one of respect, care, and connection. Whether this will make any difference on a societal or global level is very hard to know, yet it is worthwhile in and of itself for it will lead to our own liberation. I often remember Bob Marley's words in 'Redemption song': 'Emancipate yourself from mental slavery; none but ourselves can free our minds.' These words could have been said by the Buddha 2,500 years ago. My own teacher coined the aphorism 'awareness is revolutionary': we might not be able to change the world, but we can change ourselves, and this is where we must begin. In the long term the world will survive – whether it will survive with us or not is highly questionable. To understand the world in a mythical way means that we honour and respect it, that we understand that we are dependent upon it, not it upon us. The world has seen many species come and go, many climatic and cataclysmic changes; it might be that humanity manifesting as a self-conscious species will not last very long. What concerns us here is that we can confront our own sense of hopelessness, and explore how we can change that into a sense of meaning and purpose.

To be grounded is to come into connection with how we really feel in relation to the world. This might mean, and probably will mean, that we will have to confront our own grief about how the world is, but, unless we are prepared to do that, no real deep change is possible. As technology and science give us more and more fascinating toys to play with, we are in danger of disappearing into a virtual world – a world that promises connectivity but delivers alienation. I do not wish to be pessimistic here. I do not wish to align myself with hopelessness, for I believe that it is possible for us individually to come out of this dream, possible to both confront the difficulties that face us and move towards something more sustainable, humane, and hopeful. Here is a poem by Hafiz, the fourteenth-century Sufi poet:

The gift
by Hafiz

We have not come here to take prisoners
But to surrender ever more deeply
to freedom and joy.

We have not come into this exquisite world
to hold ourselves hostage from love.
Run, my dear,
from anything that may not strengthen
your precious budding wings,

Run like hell, my dear,
from anyone likely to put a sharp knife
into the sacred, tender vision
of your beautiful heart.

We have a duty to befriend
those aspects of obedience
that stand outside of our house
and shout to our reason
'oh please, oh please
come out and play.'

For we have not come here to take prisoners,
or to confine our wondrous spirits,
But to experience ever and ever more deeply
our divine courage, freedom,
and Light![9]

So much of Sufi poetry has a very contemporary feel because it is concerned with the liberation of the human heart, and this concern remains as relevant today as it always has been. It is the same concern that motivated the Buddha, and it is the same concern that motivates us. While it is often obscured, hidden under the concerns of everyday life, nevertheless it remains and comes to the surface whenever we stop. So grounding is also a kind of stopping: it is allowing ourselves to find our courage to come fully into our hearts.

The Myth of Meditation

Chapter five

....

The diamond throne

I hope we are beginning to see that grounding is not about, or not just about, relaxing and feeling comfortable. It is not something that we just do as a preliminary to getting on with our real meditation. It is an essential part of meditation that will deepen over the months and years of practice. The exercises in this book are here just to indicate the type of thing we might do; they are in no way exhaustive of the possibilities, of ways we might individually find to feel connected to ourselves and to the world. What they do strongly imply is that there is an essential relationship between ourselves and the world. What I mean by this is simply that we are part of the world and that our connection to this world is through our own bodies and minds.

It is said that the Buddha gained enlightenment, or awakening, seated under a great tree, and in turn this bodhi tree was at the centre of the universe. According to myth, this tree had grown at the place where the universe first took form, where it coalesced from its gaseous state. This spot is known as the diamond throne, and it is at this place, under the bodhi tree, that all the Buddhas are said to have gained awakening. We are not meant to take this literally; rather, it is to be understood metaphorically or poetically as indicating the central importance of awakening. We could say that, whenever we sit fully present, we are ourselves sitting on the diamond throne.

 Taking our place in the world

Sitting in your meditation posture, have a sense of the parts of your body that are in direct contact with the cushion and mat on which you are sitting. Taking your time, begin to breathe into this sense of contact with the earth. Just being aware of the sense of contact on the in-breath and on the out-breath, notice whether it feels different when you are breathing in or breathing out. While trying to stay with the actual sensations of contact between your body and the ground, also begin to imagine that, as you breathe in, you are drawing up the earth energy into your body, and, as you breathe out, imagine letting go of any tension in your body into the ground under you. Imagine that the earth is quite happy to give her energy to you and also to absorb the tension that you are holding back into herself.

When we do this kind of meditation, using our imagination, we should not take it too seriously, by which I mean we should not try to force anything to happen. It is a kind of light imagining: we are not wilfully trying to make something happen, and we do not worry too much about whether it is actually happening or not.

So we are just staying with an awareness of our breath and the sense of contact we have with the earth under us. Try and imagine that your connection to the earth is going further and further down into the earth itself: you are drawing up energy from ever deeper in the earth, and at the same time on the out-breath you are letting go of any tension that you feel in your body into the earth. Allow your attention to focus more and more on the area of your pelvic floor, particularly the perineum: imagine that you are drawing up the energy through this point and that this energy is moving up through the core of your body just in front of your spinal column. See how high the energy goes: maybe into the belly or your heart area, or even right up to the crown of your head. It is important not to try to force this: as I say, we do it quite lightly. Do this for about 15 minutes, and then stop trying to do anything at all – just sit for a few more minutes doing nothing.

With all the exercises that we will be doing in this book it is a good idea to end them with a short period of just sitting, a few minutes of doing nothing, just keeping the posture and absorbing the experience.

In this exercise, we are beginning to emphasize the importance of bringing our awareness down in the body. In the Zen tradition, a tradition that very much emphasizes meditation, there is a phenomenon known as 'Zen sickness'. This seems to be brought about by being overwilful in our approach to meditation. This sickness is a condition where meditation breaks down, and might also cause a sense of great lassitude. The antidote to this is to pay more attention to the lower parts of the body, the body from the waist down. Although the traditional texts on this condition are somewhat esoteric, it seems to be related to meditating from the head. Bringing the awareness down into the lower body ensures that we do not meditate in a way that causes tension and stress. More generally, and in line with the approach to meditation we are taking here, we can think of the lower body as holding the unconscious, or, we could even say, our own underworld. In addition, in most energy systems a connection to the earth, that is a fundamental sense of security and belonging, is associated with the lowest chakra, the base chakra, which is located at the perineum. Although I am not in favour of taking these types of energy systems in a literal way, I do think they indicate something important. It is my experience that, unless the lower body – particularly the area of the pelvis, sexual organs, perineum, anus, and base of the spine – is included, meditation remains quite shallow and ungrounded.

We need to establish right from the beginning of our practice that meditation is something that we do with the whole body: it should be understood as a physical practice, albeit a subtle one. This of course does not exclude mind – rather it puts it into its proper context. We do not have a mind that is in any way separate from the body. We need to understand the phenomenon of consciousness as arising from the whole of the psychophysical complex. When we look at mind from an evolutionary perspective, we see that it has arisen out of the body. The mind allows us to map both the internal and the external world, and in doing so allows us to act appropriately within the environment in which we find ourselves. Most of this constant adapting of the body to the environment is unconscious. In human beings and other higher animals, however, the extraordinary phenomenon of self-consciousness has arisen. Biologists and psychologists are increasingly talking in terms of emergence. In this way of understanding evolution, the interpenetration of the environment with the individual animal or plant is emphasized. This means that the animal is not understood as just adapting to the external environment, but understood as co-evolving with it. What is interesting for us in these ideas is that they suggest that the individual is deeply and inexorably grounded in their environment, and of course they are part of the environment for everything else. When we look at something like a tree, with its roots going down deep into the ground, it is quite easy to understand that it cannot really be separated from the field in which it grows, and that it is itself an environment for countless other organisms such as insects, birds, and so on. It is quite clear that it grows out of the world and in the world. This seems perhaps less obvious for us, as we can move around and are seemingly relatively independent from our environment. But of course this is not true: we are just as dependent and part of the world as anything else. However, our highly developed mind and body, which give rise to this phenomenon we call consciousness, give us a sense of separateness and independence. Here is a Derek Walcott poem, 'Earth':

Earth
by Derek Walcott

Let the day grow on you upward
through your feet,
the vegetable knuckles,

to your knees of stone,
until by evening you are a black tree;
feel, with evening,

the swifts thicken your hair,
the new moon rising out of your forehead,
and the moonlit veins of silver

running from your armpits
like rivulets under white leaves.
Sleep, as ants

cross over your eyelids.
You have never possessed anything
as deeply as this.

This is all you have owned
from the first outcry
through forever;
you can never be dispossessed.[10]

This poem evokes our intimacy with the world, and it is this intimacy that we are concerned with rather than any scientific explanation. Ever since the 1960s, it has been quite popular to point out the increasing convergence between certain aspects of modern science and what we might call the mystic or meditative traditions. However, in a sense this is really rather irrelevant: as we have already noted, science reveals the world in a particular way, and the fact that science comes to conclusions that are strikingly similar to those that mystics have in the past reached through inner exploration surprises us only because we have such faith in science while we tend to be very dismissive of wisdom traditions that do not neatly fit into the scientific and technological paradigms.

I think it is important that we do not regard science as the only yardstick of truth. No number of neuroscientists or psychologists are likely to match Shakespeare for insight into human nature. There are many things in the world that cannot be weighed or measured, which are outside of the province of science. For science to be the only criterion through which we validate such things as meditation is to give science an authority it does not have. Of course, it is possible to put receptors on people's heads and measure their brainwaves as they meditate, but to see this as proving meditation, rather than relying on 2,500 years of human experience, is frankly rather ridiculous.

I think it is important to understand that, while many people are attracted to Buddhism because it seems to be quite rational, which indeed it is, it is not rational in the sense that it is necessarily scientifically true. Rather, it is rational in the sense that it conforms to people's real lived experience. Buddhism does not offer an abstract, metaphysical theory about how things are, which can be proved or disproved; rather, it is the accumulated wisdom of many generations of practitioners, people who have tested its ideas and practices against their own experience. While science has offered extraordinary insights into the material world, there is no microscope powerful enough to see into the depths of the human heart. As is often the case, the poets say it best; here is Miroslav Holub, who was himself a respected immunologist:

What the heart is like
by Miroslav Holub

Officially the heart
is oblong, muscular,
and filled with longing.

But anyone who has painted the heart knows
that it is also

spiked like a star
and sometimes bedraggled
like a stray dog at night
and sometimes powerful
like an archangel's drum.

And sometimes cube-shaped
like a draughtsman's dream
and sometimes gaily round
like a ball in a net.

And sometimes like a thin line
and sometimes like an explosion.

And in it is
only a river,
a weir
and at most one little fish
by no means golden.

More like a grey
jealous
loach.

It certainly isn't noticeable
at first sight.

Anyone who has painted the heart knows
that first he had to
discard his spectacles,
his mirror,
throw away his fine-point pencil
and carbon paper

and for a long while
walk
outside.[11]

As with many good poems, this one has a rather unsettling line: 'more like a grey jealous loach'. Often people react a little to that line – they don't like the idea that at the very centre of the heart is this rather unimpressive little fish. I wonder what Holub was trying to get at here? In a way, Buddhism goes even further and says there is not even a little fish in there, there is nothing at all. But, paradoxically, it is this realization that liberates us. The line that comes before, 'and in it is only a river', seems to me to come very close to what Buddhism is saying, and indeed also certain Greek philosophers such as Heraclitus with his emphasis on flux – and no doubt modern science will at some point verify this insight, and we will all be able to sleep peacefully in our beds.

 ## Grounding in the posture

Take up your meditation posture, making sure that you are as comfortable as possible. To start with, perhaps take a few deep breaths, breathing in through the nose and out through your mouth, making sure that you breathe out all the air. Let the breath return to normal. Just notice whatever sounds there are around you. Do not strain to hear them – just notice how they naturally arise in your consciousness; you do not have to make any special effort. Have a sense of the world around you. You probably have your eyes closed, but just imagine the world outside of the room or building you are in. Slowly let your imagination spread out into the city or town, into the countryside, further and further, a bit like zooming out on Google Maps. You do not necessarily have to have a clear visual image: it is more a matter of feel, having a sense of the world all around you, and having the sense that you are sitting in the world.

Then imagine that the earth you are sitting on not only spreads outwards but also goes down. Imagine it going down, deeper and deeper. Have the sense that it really does go down thousands of miles below you; have a sense that in its centre it is molten, a core of energy. We have the sense of sitting in the world and on the world. This is your ground, and above you is the sky. Whenever we meditate, above us is the sky, and below us is the earth. This is our basic context, and we come back to this whenever we get lost; we come back to the world, the earth, and the sky.

Breathe in and out knowing that the earth is below you and the sky is above you. Begin to focus in on the sensations of contact between you and the earth. Take your time: there is no rush. As before, notice your breathing, and on the in-breath begin to imagine that you are drawing up the energy of the earth into the bones of the pelvis, into the whole pelvic area. At the same time imagine that you are drawing down the sky energy. You might want to remember that, when you were born, your skull was still open, and imagine that this part of your skull is slightly thinner bone, even translucent, and through it, as you breathe in, you are drawing down the energy of the sky – it is kind of falling down through your body. You are drawing in both the earth energy and the sky energy. Be careful to keep this light. As before, we are not trying to force anything to happen – it is a light imagining. You are imagining there is energy coming up through the perineum and the bones of the pelvis, rising out perhaps just in front of the spinal column or through the spine itself. At the same time, you are imagining a drawing down from the sky. Just see what this feels like, what your imagination does with these images. See how the energy of the body is affected. What does it feel like to imagine the earth and sky meeting in your heart?

Now while you are doing this, also imagine the tail bone, the sitting bones, the floor of the pelvis, being drawn down as if they have a natural affinity with the earth. At the same time, imagine the crown of your head being drawn upwards, and in between your head and your pelvis imagine your spine. Imagine your spine as it is, not just made of hard bone but also with soft and spongy tissue, fluid, delicate nerves, and so on. Imagine it as alive in your body, imagine it going right up inside your head, level with the two little indentations just behind the ear lobes. So it is going from the centre of your head, through your heart centre, through your belly, and fusing on to your pelvis. Imagine your spine as a line of electric current in your body, connecting your skull directly down to the bones of the pelvis. What we are trying to do here is to encourage a sense of real vitality in the body, a sense of energy moving freely in the body, and a sense that the body is intimately connected with the world, with the earth, and with the sky.

Earth and sky can be understood as two basic archetypal symbols. Broadly speaking, we can think of the earth as feminine, supportive, holding. We might also relate it with soul. Sky is masculine, open, and expansive and might be associated with spirit. Of course, archetypes are never simple and always contain contradictions within themselves. However, it is clear that we need both of these qualities, that of the earth and the sky, in order to meditate effectively. My suspicion is that most meditators have rather too much sky, that is to say they want to ascend, go up into spaciousness and clarity. People often take up meditation with the idea that they will rise above their everyday woes. It is quite common for people to have a fantasy where they see themselves as looking down compassionately on the suffering of others, while they themselves are in a state of blissful equanimity.

This is to some extent the fantasy that the West has about the East, the fantasy that we have about the Buddha. But when we look at the Buddha's life, we see that it was a very active one: he spent his time walking from village to village, town to town, engaging with all sorts of people; along with meditating, he did a great deal of teaching, as well as begging for his own food. He walked great distances and was very active in helping others. He was very practical in making his teachings accessible to all types of people. For just a few months in the year, during the rainy season, he would settle in one place; the rest of the time he was constantly on the move, constantly making himself available to others from all walks of life. He was often called upon to settle various types of disputes and to give advice on all types of issues, from matters of state to those involving the everyday lives of ordinary people faced with bereavement or other types of suffering. In short, he was very much part of the society in which he lived and became a renowned teacher and guide.

His life gives us a vivid example of what these days would be called engaged Buddhism. It shows us very clearly that his understanding of the spiritual life was not one where we are removed or above the everyday world, but rather one where wonder is intimately connected with life. Meditation is not something we do in order to be separated from the everyday concerns of life; rather, it is something we do in order to be able to act creatively within life. While it might be true that, at certain stages of its development, Buddhism became rather remote from the concerns of the world with the development of vast monastic institutions, this was many years after the life of the Buddha. It is very useful to have certain periods where one can concentrate exclusively on such things as meditation by going on retreat, but for most of us the real challenge is to integrate meditation into our daily lives. We are not trying to forget the world, but to find ways in which to live and act creatively within the world.

Grounding is a grounding in the world, grounding in everyday lived experience. As I have already mentioned, it is in particular grounding in suffering. For it is our sense of dissatisfaction that makes us turn away from our lives. The exercises we have done so far should be seen as indicating the kind of work that we need to do in order to begin to truly ground. There are of course many other things that we can do, and we should not see these exercises as in any way exhaustive of the possibilities: they are merely indicating the kind of thing that can be useful. You should feel free to make up your own, to do what comes naturally, so to speak. What is important is that you get a sense of what it feels like to be more grounded. It might not feel blissful or even always very comfortable, because it means being prepared to sit with difficult mental states and even some physical discomfort. What it should mean is that you feel more connected with your body, your feelings, and the world.

Part 2

Turning towards

Chapter six

An elephant's stance

I want to begin this second part of the book by acknowledging that the phrase 'turning towards' has been borrowed from Chögyam Trungpa, who was one of the major figures in the establishment of Tibetan Buddhism in the West. He is quoted by a number of his senior students as often saying, 'Always turn towards, never turn away' – indeed some of his students have gone so far as to say that the whole of his approach to Buddhism could be summed up in this seemingly simple phrase.

I do not know if it is true, but I've heard it said that, when elephants look at something, they turn their whole body to do so. And this is the image that I have for this phrase. For me, turning towards suggests something physical as much as psychological. It means that we turn to face the situation squarely and fully, and we can contrast it with the idea of turning away. It seems to me important that we understand this as an image as much as an idea. For me, an image is somewhat deeper than an idea, or perhaps, rather, ideas have their roots in image. When we understand something deeply in this way, approach something through an image, it has a different feel to it, it is more embodied. I like the elephant – the elephant is nothing if not embodied. Here is a poem by Christopher Reid that I have used recently when talking about the idea of turning towards while teaching on retreat.

A scattering
by Christopher Reid

I expect you've seen the footage: elephants,
finding the bones of one of their own kind
dropped by the wayside, picked clean by scavengers
and the sun, then untidily left there,
    decide to do something about it.

But what, exactly? They can't, of course,
reassemble the old elephant magnificence;
they can't even make a tidier heap. But they can
hook up bones with their trunks and chuck them
    this way and that way. So they do.
    And their scattering has an air
of deliberate ritual, ancient and necessary.
Their great size, too, makes them the very
embodiment of grief, while the play of their trunks
    lends sprezzatura.
    Elephants puzzling out
the anagram of their own anatomy,
elephants at their abstracted lamentations –
may their spirit guide me as I place
    my own sad thoughts in new, hopeful arrangements.[12]

This poem, the title poem from a collection written in response to the death of the poet's wife, is a wonderful example of what it might be to turn towards one of life's most difficult experiences, the loss of a loved and long-time partner. I find the image of the elephants hooking up the bones of their dead very strong, and the way Christopher Reid uses this image to turn towards his own thoughts equally moving.

We should not think that turning towards is really that different from our first stage of grounding. The turning towards comes naturally out of the grounding and is really an intensification of it. Indeed, it is not really satisfactory to call them stages at all, which might imply a kind of linear progression towards a particular end. I think the idea of progress is very deeply ingrained in the modern mind: we want something to be leading somewhere, we are obsessed with the idea of growth. It is this obsession with progress and growth that underpins our society, but often it is little more than greed. And, in turn, this greed is in itself a response to fear – it is one way we have of turning away from our own mortality, as if the constant accumulation of more will somehow save us from our fate. If we want to truly turn towards what is, one of the major things we have to overcome is this constant craving for things to be

                                               The Myth of Meditation

better, to have more. As meditators, we are interested in what is, and, if we meditate always wanting something more – a higher state of consciousness, more clarity, insight or enlightenment – we are never really with our actual experience: we are always moving away from it. We are then, in Buddhist terms, in the grip of some form of craving, albeit subtle.

Of course, we cannot be too absolute about this: there is probably nearly always some subtle craving operating; there might be rare moments when this is completely absent, but on the whole some craving will be there. We should not worry about this unduly – we must learn not to take ourselves too seriously, particularly when it comes to 'spiritual' practice. When we take ourselves too seriously, this is a sign that we are coming from an egocentric point of view. Dōgen, the thirteenth-century Zen master, is often quoted as saying, 'we must make one mistake after another'.[13] Zen masters are notoriously difficult to interpret. Nevertheless, I like this: it gives me hope. I think one of the most important things in practice is to develop a certain robustness, a kind of confidence that is based on being realistic about oneself.

One of the things I have always responded to in Buddhism is that it begins with a very realistic notion of people: it frankly states that we are driven by greed and hatred, and this is because we have a fundamental and very deep-rooted delusion. This delusion or ignorance is around the area of our own self, or what we would now call ego self. It is not primarily an intellectual mistake, that we believe in an unchanging permanent self, although this might well be the case; it is more that we behave as if we were immortal – we behave as if we were the centre of the world. This might not be a problem if it did not make us so unhappy. As we have already noted, Buddhism begins with suffering; this is to say, it begins with what our actual experience of life is. If you were actually completely happy and content, if you did not feel that there was anything missing from your life, you probably would not have read this far. According to traditional accounts of the Buddha's life, he was born into privilege and lived a very comfortable and cultured life. Nevertheless, he was driven by a sense of dissatisfaction to embark upon his spiritual quest. So the suffering that Buddhism talks about does not have to be extreme. Indeed, if it is too extreme one is quite likely to think that there are other solutions; for instance, if you are in extreme poverty, it is likely that you will feel that an improvement in your material circumstances offers a solution to your suffering, and no doubt such an improvement might well alleviate it to some extent. However, when life is objectively pleasant, there is often still this itch, this indefinable sense that things are not quite right. What Buddhism is offering is a way of working with our existential situation. At the risk of becoming too abstract, we could say that Buddhism is concerned with a kind of existential alignment between us and the way things really are, and, until this alignment is achieved, there will always be a sense of being out of place in the world. We are told in the old accounts of the Buddha's life that, when he visited his followers, perhaps in the forest, he would always ask after their material well-being first: did they have enough food, adequate shelter, medicine, and so on? It is as if a certain level of everyday well-being needs to be in place before one can really apply oneself to meditation and other practices that would help to overcome this more subtle but deep existential need.

While it is gratifying to see that mindfulness and other Buddhist practices are being used to address issues of physical and psychological suffering, it is also important to realize that at the heart of Buddhism is an analysis of the existential suffering of human beings. Of course, there is no absolute distinction between these types of suffering, and there is a chronic need to address suffering on all its levels. Nevertheless, here we are concerned primarily with this existential aspect of suffering that can be understood as at the very core of suffering. I have a good friend who is a very skilled psychotherapist, and one thing he often says is that, if suffering has a sense of meaning to it, it is bearable, but without the sense that there is some meaning in our suffering it becomes unbearable. This does not mean we should have some grandiose ideas about what we are doing. It does mean, however, that we are very fortunate that material circumstances allow us to address what is at the very heart of human dissatisfaction. The Tibetans emphasize how fortunate it is to have been born a human being. They say this because

The Myth of Meditation

it is only as a human being that we have this opportunity to address our relationship to reality.

Another way of talking about meditation is in relation to the cultivation of a sense of meaning. Personally, this has come to be the way that I understand why I am a meditator. I have been teaching beginners meditation for over twenty-five years, and one of the most common questions I am asked is, 'Why do you meditate?' It is of course a very reasonable question, one that I feel bound to respond to as honestly as possible. While I will point out that it helps with such things as stress and anxiety, for myself I have to tell people that I meditate because I find it intrinsically meaningful. Now this is really quite a hard thing to articulate, but when I am sitting I feel that I am in relationship to myself in a way that I rarely achieve at other times. It is like coming home, a sense of real intimacy. It is not that anything spectacular happens. Of course meditation can sometimes be dramatic and spectacular – in my case that is very rare – but, even though nothing dramatic happens, there is a deep sense of satisfaction in just being with oneself in a wholehearted, quiet sort of way. Over the years, less and less seems to happen in my meditation practice. However, far from becoming bored with it, I find it increasingly engaging. Perhaps some of this is down to age. I am not sure, but I think there is something more fundamental going on here – I think that this kind of resting within oneself with little mental activity is a natural state that is intrinsically nourishing.

We have in the modern age come to take for granted that the mind is perpetually busy, but I do not think this is the natural state of the mind at all, far from it. Before the Industrial Revolution, before the advent of radio, television, and so on, people's minds were not stimulated in the way they are now – they were not always active. There is of course no way to prove that, but my experience of going on solitary retreat has shown me that the mind, when not constantly stimulated, naturally begins to slow down. We realize that we do not have to be 'thinking' all of the time, that it is quite possible for the mind to be in a clear, ready state, as if the mind is just at rest, being within the body, available when needed.

This brings us to one of the most basic confusions, which is the confusion between thinking and awareness. Thinking is not the same as awareness. Thinking is one possible function of mind; usually, however, thinking rather than strengthening awareness tends to obscure it. There is also a further complication. Most of our thinking we are barely conscious of, barely aware of. When you come to meditate, you become very familiar with this. You notice that your mind is more or less constantly active: one thought follows another, they just happen unbidden by us. So this is mental activity, but is it really thinking? We can use the term 'thinking' to imply something conscious, something that we do on purpose to address a particular problem, or achieve a particular end. This is of course an entirely legitimate use of the mind, when we are consciously engaged in using the mind, using the thinking faculty of the mind. So this is one thing, but the constant and endless chatter that we experience when we try to meditate is quite another thing. It sometimes seems as if this kind of chatter begins when we begin to try and meditate, but this is not really the case. The truth is that it is going on all the time, and it is only when we try to do something simple, like bringing the awareness into the body or onto the breath, that we notice this constant chatter.

One reason for this overactivity of mind is just that we are overstimulated: from the moment we get up to the moment we go to bed, we are bombarded with sound and image constantly occupying the mind in a frenetic and fragmented kind of way. When this sort of activity is going on in the mind, what we might call awareness is greatly impaired. In order to be in a mindful state, that is a state in which we are aware of what is actually going on both inside and outside of ourselves, we need to be relatively calm, and our minds need to be free of anxiety, planning, scheming, or whatever else it is that tends to occupy us so much.

Chapter seven

....

Embracing the depths

When we first begin to meditate, our minds will tend to be full of thoughts. Often, when we look at what the nature of these thoughts is, we will see that they are driven by emotion, such as anxiety, fear, hate, desire, and so on. When we come to turning towards, it is not so much particular thoughts that we are interested in, but rather what is beneath them, particularly the underlying emotions that drive them. For us to be able to do this, we have to be grounded. This is because our emotions are felt rather than thought, so, unless we are reasonably grounded, that is in relationship to our bodies, we are not going to be able to contact the emotions that are giving rise to our obsessive mental activity.

Turning towards is the process by which we become more aware of the full range of our experience. Normally our experience is dominated by one aspect, that is our mental activity in terms of our thoughts. However, our potential experience is always far richer than this: it includes a whole world of sensation and emotion. We can think of this as usually being just below the surface of our awareness. We are not actually able to be aware of very much else at the same time, as our heads are filled with mental chatter. So, if our minds are caught up in this kind of thinking, we will not be very aware of other aspects of our experience, such as underlying emotions, which give rise to this thinking in the first place. This is an important point, so I hope it is clear. Let us restate it in a slightly different way: we can say that the depth of our experience is obscured by the surface activity of our minds.

One of the fundamental things we are trying to do is to readdress an imbalance in the way we experience ourselves. What we are trying to do is to bring our awareness down into the body.

Of course, this is just a way of talking and cannot be taken too literally, but it is a useful metaphor. Let's take the experience of anxiety, which is so common today. When we are anxious, we are usually aware of that because of the kind of thoughts that we are having: we might be compulsively thinking about whatever it is that seems to be the source of our anxiety. When we sit in meditation, we need to acknowledge these thoughts and, at the same time, very gently try and get below them. So what is below them? There is no simple answer to this question, but what I am suggesting is that there will be bodily tension, uncomfortable feelings, and perhaps even images. The source of our anxiety is not the particular thoughts that we are having, but rather something deeper. As long as we are caught in the particular thoughts, trying to think ourselves out of it, we will do little more than exacerbate the problems that we are having. In a way, we are not trying to do anything about our thoughts at all; rather, we are trying to allow our awareness to relax down into the body, down below the surface of our experience. I say 'we are trying to', but this is not really a satisfactory way of putting it, and here we confront one of the paradoxes of meditation: what we are doing is just paying attention to our experience and trusting that this taking care will in time reveal what is really there. To the thinking mind, to the ego, this is a very frustrating process. It is frustrating because it cannot be willed – we cannot make it happen. To the degree that we try and make it happen, we will still be caught up with the thinking mind, so it is much more a matter of just relaxing into our experience. However, this is quite a particular type of relaxing – it is not just doing nothing; rather, it is paying attention. And, to come back full circle, in order to pay attention in the type of way that we are speaking of here, we first have to be grounded. As we have seen already, to be grounded means to be in an active and imaginative relationship with both our immediate surroundings and our body.

We are now ready to turn towards, but what is it exactly that we are turning towards? In broad terms we can say that we are turning towards soul. As we have already seen, this cannot be closely defined. We are turning towards something that is below our normal level of experience. We are most interested

The Myth of Meditation

in those vague feelings, fleeting images, ideas that are just out of reach. In order for this to be possible, there has to be a certain stability and a genuine interest. As we have stressed, grounding provides this basic stability. Once this has been established, we also need a method for maintaining it.

So here is a version of the Mindfulness of Breathing, a classic Buddhist meditation practice. I prefer to call this meditation 'the mindfulness of our breathing body'. I make this distinction because I think there is always a danger of treating the breath as if it were an object that has little to do with us, whereas the truth is, without the breath we would not exist at all.

 ## The mindfulness of our breathing body

Take up your meditation posture. Do not rush: just take your time making sure you are as comfortable as possible. With your spine upright, have a sense of the earth below you and the sky above you. Do not try and block out your surroundings. Rather, try and just relax into the situation you find yourself in. Even if there is a little noise, just be aware of it in an open way, not resisting it but rather allowing it to support you to be present. Do what you need to do to relax your face, hands, and feet. When you are ready, just notice your natural breath. Do this in quite a casual sort of way: do not grab at it – it is always there, always available to your awareness, so there is no need to worry about losing it. So we are just going to follow the natural rhythm of our breath, being aware when we are breathing out and when we are breathing in.

Once you have settled onto your breath, begin to count to yourself, marking the end of each out-breath. Breathing in and out, count one, and continue to count until you have counted to ten breaths. When you get to ten, start again at one. So we are just marking the out-breath by counting. However, the weight of our attention is on the breath, not on the counting. This is not an exercise in being able to count. Do this first stage for about ten minutes, and then change the place where you are counting to the beginning of the breath. So now you are marking the beginning of the breath, anticipating your breath, using the counting to set the mind onto the breath at the beginning of each one, counting the same way, in sets of ten. In both this and the preceding stage, if you lose count just begin again at one – do not waste time trying to figure out what number you were on: if you are not sure, just start again at one. In both of these stages, you only have to be aware of the breaths one at a time: the counting breaks up the breath into one cycle at a time. Do this for about the same amount of time as the first stage, and then just let the counting fade away.

In the next stage, we are interested in trying to keep a continuity of awareness. So now we are just sitting with the breath with no counting to support us. Just sit with your breath for about ten minutes. To bring the meditation to an end, just stop trying to do anything at all, other than keeping the posture.

Some of you might be familiar with this practice having a fourth stage, in which you focus on a particular sensation within the breath, often at the tip of the nose. When we do this, we are exploring the concentration aspects of the practice, but here we just want to develop a general stability of awareness using the breath, which is quite open and broad, so we are omitting this last stage.

Whenever I meditate, I always use the breath. This is because the breath is always there, it is part of our fundamental experience of being alive, it gives a basic stability to our awareness, and it encourages us to take notice of the body, which in turn makes our emotions more available to us.

Once we have cultivated this intimate relationship with our breath, which might take quite some time, we are in a position to begin to turn towards the other aspects of our experience; the breath becomes the space in which they are arising. It is as if our experience of ourselves and the world happens within the context of the breath. If we try to turn towards our experience without the breath supporting us, the likelihood is that we will just become entangled and lost in whatever the experience is. We can see the breath as bringing a sense of spaciousness and clarity to our exploration, and in this sense the breath is synonymous with awareness. While this may not make that much sense on an intellectual level, it is what happens – or can happen – experientially.

I do want to stress that we are not treating the breath as an object. Often, when this type of practice is presented, the breath is referred to as the object of concentration. While there might not be anything wrong with this if our aim is to become concentrated, that is to get into higher states of consciousness, this is really not what we are trying to do here. It might be that you become naturally absorbed in the breath and find yourself in quite a different state of mind from your normal experience, which is fine – don't try and stop this: just go with it in a natural relaxed way and see where it takes you. Becoming more absorbed can be a very pleasant and useful thing to happen. However, in this approach the emphasis is on just trying to get enough stability to be able to notice what is happening in our bodies and hearts.

I have noticed that some people are very adept at getting concentrated and, while this is a positive thing in a general sense, we also need to beware using it to avoid our experience. I have known people who are 'strong' meditators in this sense of easily getting into concentrated states, but who have the idea that meditation has nothing to do with their normal experience, nothing to do with their psychology, and they use it as a way of getting 'above' their normal selves. It should be clear by now that we are not exploring this approach to meditation here.

This is a rather controversial area among meditation teachers, and it is only right that I should point out that many other teachers will disagree with me. Within the Buddhist tradition I am part of, some practitioners have emphasized concentration and these higher states of mind, and this clearly has its place in the tradition. However, I have also met people who, after many years of meditating with concentration as their goal, find that their practice breaks down, and they are left with a dissatisfied feeling that this approach to meditation has left untouched deeper parts of themselves.

This indeed is at the heart of the distinction we have already made between spirit and soul. Rather crudely, I would characterize the type of meditation that aims for 'concentration above all else' as its goal as placing too much emphasis on spirit. It can become wilful and overly concerned with making spiritual 'progress'. To remind us of our quote from Wallace Stevens, 'the way through the world is more difficult to find than the way beyond it'. We are not concerned here with rising above ourselves or the world, in leaving the body and emotions behind, and going into some kind of spiritual and rather abstract place where nothing touches us.

However, I do not want to be dismissive of these higher states: they can bring much joy and inspiration, and as such can be rejuvenating and encouraging. It is more that, if we make them the point of meditation practice, we run the risk in the long term of either losing interest or becoming disillusioned. This is because there is a tendency for these states, when unchecked, to be based on a subtle form of craving, and the nature of craving is that we always want more and we can never get enough. In addition, they are relative, by which I mean that, if we are always becoming absorbed to a certain level, after a while this will become familiar and no longer give us the gratification it once did so we will want more. Sometimes it is useful just to allow yourself to go into higher states when they naturally occur. I do not want to be dogmatic about this: a balance of spirit with soul is useful. However, as I see it, it is only when we become interested in actual mundane experience, in the nuts and bolts, the blood and guts of our experience, that things really become interesting and rewarding.

There is another distinction that I think we need to make in relationship to the possibility of experiencing higher states of mind. Broadly speaking, I think that these are useful in so far as they are reached through the body. There seems to be an increasing recognition of the phenomenon sometimes called 'spiritual bypassing', where spiritual practice is used to avoid difficult aspects of our own psychology. While this is quite a complicated area, I believe that, if practice is firmly rooted in awareness of body, sensations, and the emotions, we will avoid falling into this trap. Also, it is important to cultivate the underlying attitude that we are interested in what *is* happening rather than having preconceived ideas about what we *think* we should be experiencing. I find myself stressing this more and more as a meditation teacher. When people talk about their meditation, they nearly always say it was either a 'good meditation' or a 'bad meditation', or words to that effect. I do understand what they mean, but these days I try always to pick them up on what they are saying, because for me it implies an underlying attitude, an attitude that is not helpful to meditation.

Suzuki, in his wonderful book *Zen Mind, Beginner's Mind*, has an essay in which he talks about there being three types of horses – excellent ones, good ones, and bad ones – and a bad horse has to feel the whip's sting to the marrow of its bones before it learns to run properly. But he suggests that, in the end, it is best to be a bad horse – that things that are hard to learn, that take great effort, that we find very difficult, are in the long run the most valuable. I think it is fair to say that sometimes more difficult meditations are the most valuable.

We have talked quite a lot about the necessity of coming into relationship with our suffering, and when we find ourselves in a difficult meditation we are presented with a real opportunity to work with or turn away. If we have learned the knack of sitting in a blissed-out state, head slightly pulled back, disconnected from our body with a beneficent smile on our face, we are probably not really turning towards – we are involved in what we have called spiritual bypassing. In traditional Buddhism, the meditational stage before bliss is known as rapture, and rapture is described largely in terms of physical pleasure, that is to say it is experienced in the body, so this gives us a good clue that we have to go through the body in order to achieve 'higher' states that are not based on alienated awareness. By and large, I do not personally feel it is very profitable to get too concerned with outcomes in meditation, that is with trying to achieve these high states per se. If they occur naturally we should enjoy them, for there is no doubt that they can be beneficial, but this is very different from making them the sole raison d'être of meditation.

I want to come back to the image of turning towards. As I have said, for me this is a very physical image, and sometimes we will notice that we literally turn away from what we find threatening or unpleasant. A physical turning away is of course an extreme example, and usually our turning away is not so obvious to others or ourselves. Another very common way of turning away is to make a joke of it, a kind of verbal shrug. The most common way in which we turn away, though, is simply to go into thinking. This is particularly true in meditation. By this I mean that, when something happens that we find in some way uncomfortable, instead of staying with the experience we begin to try and rationalize it away.

This is equivalent to our tendency to want to interpret dreams. When we have a disturbing dream, most of us immediately try to figure out what it might mean. What we are doing is trying to make it safe from the perspective of the ego, which feels threatened by the images and feelings that made up our dream, which are not consistent with the ego's own image of itself. It is more or less impossible not to fall into this interpretation, and likewise it is more or less impossible not to do it in meditation, at least not without a lot of experience. But, although it is difficult to stop the ego immediately kicking in and appropriating the experience for itself, this does not mean we should not be aware of its tendency. This might sound a little paradoxical, but the main point is that we should not really worry too much that we do this; rather, we should just be aware of it.

So much of what happens when we meditate in a relaxed and open way has some correspondence with what happens when we dream. In both cases, what we can call the ego loses its perpetual vigilance to some degree. When the ego begins to relax, it allows material from what we might call the unconscious, or our own underworld, to come into awareness. This rising up of material may take many forms: sensations in the body, memories from the past, seemingly meaningless images, and so on. Once this happens, we will notice that the tendency we have described above often kicks in, that is the ego wants to make sense of it, to lay claim to it in order to render it part of our normal, everyday-world experience. However, we should as far as possible just try and sit with the experience. This is quite a subtle and difficult thing to do. Ideally it involves being attentive without interfering – a kind of radical non-intervention. We do not try and hold, say, an image that arises. By which I mean we do not try and stop it changing, but we try and allow it to change on its own without prompting from the ego consciousness. We need to emphasize that this isn't really possible – at some point we will fall into trying to make sense of our experience – but nevertheless, to the extent that we can leave it to unfold under its own momentum, we should. In relation to meditation practice, this radical non-interference is at the heart of what we are calling turning towards: it is our basic method.

Outside of meditation, there are other ways of working with this material, one of which is poetry. Most good poets have the ability to allow non-conscious elements to come into their writing. Indeed, this is a common feature of most artistic processes: the artist is not completely in control of what happens. Through absorption in the process of making the art, unconscious material is allowed to become part of it. Traditionally writers call this the muse; it is as if the inspiration were coming from a source outside of the artist. The painter Francis Bacon saw the power of his work as the result of 'accident':

> In my case all painting [...] is an accident. I foresee it and
> yet I hardly ever carry it out as I foresee it. It transforms
> itself by the actual paint. I don't in fact know very often
> what the paint will do, and it does many things which are
> very much better than I could make it do.[14]

Of course, unlike art, meditation has no material product, although we might not be stretching the analogy too far in saying that the psyche is the material that we are working with. And, just as with the artist, in order to be able to allow this process to happen there has to be a basic confidence. The flip side of this is of course the great doubt that artists often experience – in the case of writers, we are familiar with the idea of writer's block. And meditators will have the equivalent: periods where they feel unable to relax into their experience, unable to contact the depths of themselves, seemingly cut off from themselves. Paradoxically, at least in the case of meditation, this often comes after a particularly strong experience of oneself. It is as if the ego, threatened by what has happened, reasserts itself with renewed vigour. Alternatively, because we have had a particularly strong experience, we try and make that reoccur, we want it again, and therefore we are overwilful in trying to repeat the experience. We will be looking at this phenomenon later, as it is a more or less inevitable consequence of what we will be calling 'seeing through'.

The archetypal psychologist James Hillman uses the term 'soul making' to describe a similar process. For Hillman, the soul as an image needs to be reclaimed by psychology, which has ironically lost its relationship to the psyche. This has occurred because of the overliteral approach that now dominates psychology, which, in so far as it has become part of 'science', has tended to lose its essential relationship with the imagination, particularly in its more mythological or archetypal aspects.

One of the main problems that we face as meditators is the loss of this aspect of imagination. For it is the imagination that allows us to feel fully part of the world: without it, we will tend to feel isolated and alone. This imaginative faculty is there in children, but often gets obscured by the demands of adult life. It can be reawakened and sustained by the arts and by nature, as well as by countless other means particular to the individual. Within meditation it is found in taking care, that is in a relaxed, attentive attitude to experience as it unfolds.

Chapter eight

······························

A call to kindness and care

The concept of care is central to this approach to meditation. Care as a philosophical concept has a long history. Socrates saw his task as 'the care of the soul', while more recently care was a pivotal notion within the thinking of existentialist philosophers such as Kierkegaard and Heidegger. Here we are using the idea of care to express a sense of kind concern. Without this, we are unable to attend to ourselves in the way we need to in order to 'hear' what the body and psyche have to say to us.

In a general sense, the best practice that we can do in order to 'turn towards' is simply to establish a sense of grounding through the active use of imagination as we have discussed already, and then to sit with the breath in a relaxed and open kind of way; this means that the attention we give to the breath is, at least once we have settled, quite light: we are not clinging to it for dear life. However, there are other things that we are going to need to do to support our ability to sit in this way.

Most importantly, we need to cultivate a high degree of emotional positivity. Within Buddhism, kindness towards both ourselves and others has always occupied a central place, alongside that of mindfulness or awareness. This is because awareness alone is not really enough – it is rather like a bird with only one wing – in the end we will come to see that both these wings of practice are in fact identical, but we nevertheless need them both. We can see that the idea of care links these two qualities: to be aware, we need to have a sense of care towards whatever our attention is directed to. In relation to our own experience, which is the main focus of our meditation, care is essential if we are going to avoid turning away from it when it does not conform to the ideas we have about ourselves. So I want to explore some of the practices that Buddhism offers to help us build up a sense of care and kindness that support our attempts to turn towards.

In a mythological or imaginative sense, Buddhism has personified these qualities in symbolic form. One of the main figures representing these qualities is Tārā, particularly the bodhisattva Green Tārā, who appears as a beautiful young maiden. She most commonly appears sitting in half-lotus, with one leg stepping down into the world, ever ready to come to our aid. We do not have the space here to go into the history of this figure, but those interested might like to seek out *The Cult of Tārā: Magic and Ritual in Tibet* by Stephan Beyer.[15] My own feeling for the figure has been based on her seeming to me to be representative of an earth goddess. Considering her in that way, we can imagine that she was there at the enlightenment of the Buddha, and witnessed his right to sit on the diamond throne. So when we sit, we can imagine her witnessing our practice. We do not of course need to imagine the figure of Tārā as such – what is important is to invite a sense of her kindness into our meditation. One of the many qualities that Tārā is said to possess is that she responds to every sincere call: there is nothing that you can do that puts you outside of her sphere of compassion – when called she comes...

Tārā, then, never turns away, and this raises the question of why it is so hard for us not to turn away. Our turning away is an attempt to avoid suffering. Although traditional Buddhism tends to suggest that our suffering is brought about by our own actions, I do not think this is quite true, or at least it has to be understood in a particular way.

The black heralds
by César Vallejo

There are knocks in life so hard... I don't know!
Knocks like God's hate; as if under them
the backwash of everything suffered
had stagnated in your soul... I don't know!

The Myth of Meditation

They are few; but they are... They open dark weals
in the keenest face, in the hardest back.
They could be the colts of wild Attilas;
or the black heralds death sends us.

They are the deep chutes of your soul Christs,
of some pretty faith Destiny blasphemes.
Those bloodied knocks are the crackling
of a loaf that burns up at the oven door.

And man... Poor man! He turns his eyes as
when a clap on the shoulder summons us;
he turns his mad eyes, and everything lived
stagnates like a guilt pond in his look.
There are knocks in life, so hard... I don't know![16]

I find this a very powerful and also difficult poem in relation
to turning towards: it confronts us with just how unbearable this
might seem at certain times in our life. It also implies that at least
some of the knocks that we have to endure come out of nowhere
and seem to have little to do with our ethical behaviour. And
this can be the case. If, for instance, our family dies in a plane
crash, it seems quite bizarre to attribute such a tragic event to our
own ethical conduct. Unfortunately, some traditional Buddhist
schools seem to imply that this is the case, that it is all our
'karma'. The Buddha, however, was clear that not everything
that happens to us can be attributed to our own willed actions,
which is what constitutes karma from a Buddhist perspective.
The Buddha, in reply to a question from a wanderer, taught:

> Those ascetics and brahmanas who hold the following
> belief: 'Whatever an individual person experiences,
> whether pleasant or painful or neither pleasant nor painful,
> all that is because of what was done in the past' – they
> exceed what one knows for oneself, and they exceed what
> is universally accepted as the truth. Therefore I say that
> those ascetics and brahmanas are wrong.[17]

Buddhism talks in terms of conditionality, saying that
everything in experience arises in dependence on conditions.

This is in fact the core teaching of the Buddha:

> This being, that becomes, from the arising of this, that
> arises; this not being, that does not become, from the
> ceasing of this, that ceases.[18]

So what else is at work in this conditionality, apart from our willed actions and our own past deeds? Sangharakshita talks of four other 'orders' or other forces that shape the world and our own lives.[19] These also have consequences for us and what we experience. These four, along with karma, are known as the five *niyama*s.

1. *Utu niyama*: the inorganic physical order

This first level of conditionality refers to inorganic matter and relates to what we would now call physics, geology, and chemistry. It would include what we call natural disasters, although with global warming it might be that human activity also plays a part. Indeed it is often the case that more than one of the *niyama*s is involved as a causal factor. However, in general this level of the physical world is not in the control of human activity, and is not caused by the karma of those who might suffer because of it, say from an earthquake, for example.

2. *Bījā niyama*: the organic physical order

This covers the laws governing organic matter, and relates to what we would know as biology. The Pali word *bījā* means 'seed', and so this level may also be understood as what we would now refer to as genetics, along with the growth and death of all organic matter such as plants and animals, as well as germs and so on.

3. *Citta niyama*: the non-volitional mental order

Citta here means 'mind', and so this level refers to the mind as a sense organ that has certain inherent abilities and limitations: it does all sorts of things that we are not aware of, such as regulating the processes in the body. It might also be subject to certain tendencies such as depression, or indeed joy, that seem to just happen.

4. *Kamma* or *karma niyama*: the volitional mental order

The first two verses of the *Dhammapada*, one of the best-known of all Buddhist texts, sum up the Buddhist idea of karma:

> All mental phenomena have mind as their forerunner; they have mind as their chief; they are mind-made. If one speaks or acts with an evil mind, 'dukkha' follows him just as the wheel follows the hoof print of the ox that draws the cart.
>
> All mental phenomena have mind as their forerunner; they have mind as their chief; they are mind-made. If one speaks or acts with a pure mind, happiness (*sukha*) follows him like a shadow that never leaves him.[20]

This level is concerned with what we might call volitional actions. Traditionally these are referred to as actions of body, speech, and mind, so here not only does what we do and say have an effect on us, but also what we think. It is important to note that Buddhism understands this as a natural law that is not dependent on the intervention of any sort of divine power. It is then just another level of the general law of conditionality, but of particular importance to us as meditators and human beings, as it is the only level that we really have some control over, and is also the level that most affects the way we go through life and the degree to which we suffer.

5. *Dhamma* or *Dharma niyama*: the order of reality

The Pali word *Dhamma* (Sanskrit *Dharma*) has many meanings. In Buddhism it is mostly used to mean the teachings of the Buddha, or indeed any teachings that are of help to us, but in this context it means something like the manifestation of reality. This order of causality relates to the way we are impacted by reality itself. We could then say that dukkha, or suffering, is a negative aspect of this, while the pull we feel towards growth, the desire we have to come into alignment with reality, is the positive side. Sometimes it is understood as an inspiration that feels as if it comes from outside of us, perhaps rather like the muse of the artist.

I won't go into these levels of conditionality in any depth, but I do feel that it is important to be aware of them, especially to be aware of the fact that they tell us that much of what happens in our own lives is not in our control. It does not matter how aware we are, we are still subject to external forces over which we have little or sometimes no control. I think that one of the more or less unconscious fantasies that many of us have on taking up a practice like meditation is that it is going to give us the power to control our lives and even perhaps to control the external world. Indeed, this wish to exert control over the world is one of the main drivers of much of human activity.

We have always sought the security that this sort of power seems to offer, whether through magic, religion, or science, or on a more mundane level through life insurance or pension funds, relationships, or family. We are constantly trying to bring the seemingly chaotic forces that influence our lives under our control. However, as the Stoics of ancient Greece and Rome understood, we can never achieve our aim: we are all subject to forces that are forever out of our control. And as the Stoics taught, the only thing that we really have control over is our own conscious actions. It follows therefore that the more aware we are, the more in touch with ourselves we are, the more control we will have over our lives. So through such things as meditation, as our awareness strengthens and expands, the more we will have a sense of ourselves as being able to make our lives worthwhile and meaningful. It is perhaps a little misleading to talk of this giving us 'control', unless we understand this control as over our own minds. What is perhaps more helpful is to say that our neurotic need to have control over what, in the end, we cannot have control over lessens, and we feel increasingly at ease in and with our lives.

As we have already noted, the more we are caught up in 'thinking', in the sense of being caught up in speculation and anxiety, the less in touch we will be with the emotions that drive this type of mental proliferation. Buddhism offers a number of traditional practices in order to address the emotional side of our experience and to gradually replace feelings of fear and anxiety with confidence and love. One of the principal practices of this kind is the practice of loving-kindness, or Mettā Bhāvanā, as it is known. This practice begins with the development of love towards ourselves, and then moves on to other people and finally all that lives. What follows is one possible way of approaching the first part of this practice, developing love and kindness towards ourselves.

 ## Calling of your name meditation

Taking the posture, spend a few minutes just tuning in to your body and developing some sense of how you feel. As always, the breath should be used to support the posture and your awareness. I often like to remember that the breath is what sustains us moment to moment, and imagine my breath as being inherently kind.

Once you feel that you have settled a little, think of your name. This might be the name you use every day, or it might be a name known only to you, or the name that your lover calls you, or a nickname. What we are looking for is the name that has the most emotional resonance for us at that time. I sometimes tell people to just listen and see what name they hear. To begin with, we will probably have to consciously say the name: do this in a loving internal voice, and after a while it might be that it is more like hearing our name called. So this is all we do, call and listen to our own name. Of course it is of vital importance that the tone of the voice is as near as possible to one of unconditional love and acceptance.

Say your name and then leave a little space to 'listen' to your reaction. It might be that after a while it seems that you are hearing someone else call your name. Often when I have done this my own voice has been replaced by another. Sometimes it has been my mother calling me in from the garden, and I find myself in touch with myself as a young child. Just be open to what happens, be curious rather than thinking it should be a particular way.

This is a simple way of exploring the heart and inviting it to open a little, using our own name as a support to paying attention to how we feel. It might be that you come up with a different idea about how you can do this. I think with all meditations it is important that you feel free to explore variations to the methods that I am putting forward. What we need to do is have a sense of what we are trying to get at with these meditations. Here we are concerned with placing an emphasis on the heart, the emotional side of our experience.

One of the reasons I like this calling of our name is that it is quite simple. I feel that, on the whole, meditation should be simple. Once practices begin to get complicated, the rational mind has too much to do and we end up losing the basic ground of our practice, which is found in a direct experience of our own bodies and feelings. Another reason I like this practice is that it seems to me to have echoes in traditional practices of chanting or calling the name of certain mythic figures such as Green Tārā, among many others. Indeed, there are a number of schools of Buddhism where chanting is the primary practice. I will say a little about using chanting later on.

So this practice of the calling of our own name is suggested here as one way of beginning to explore our feeling towards ourselves. It is one of the saddest things about our present modern culture that very many of us do not have a positive, loving feeling towards ourselves. In traditional Buddhist cultures, it is seen as a wonderful thing to have been born as a human being: it means that we have an opportunity to make conscious progress and contribute to the well-being of the world. I remember once hearing the Dalai Lama talk about when he first started teaching Westerners. He recalls being asked questions about self-esteem, and finding these questions very strange because in his own culture people did not have these problems with low self-esteem – they had been born human, and this in and of itself gave them a positive attitude. The people of Tibet have all sorts of problems to face that we do not have in the West, but they do, it seems, have a basic sense of self-worth that many of us in the West seem to struggle to attain.

I have spent a lot of time talking to people about their meditation practice. Particularly when I lead retreats, which I do a lot, people come and have a chat with me about what goes on in their meditation. Many of the problems that I encounter seem to have at their root a basic lack of self-love. When this is the case, it is very hard to make progress in meditation until this lack is addressed. Indeed we can see this sense of lack as one of the principal characteristics of our culture, one of the main drivers of neurotic and self-destructive activities.

Meditation is one way we have of trying to address this problem, but it is not a quick fix. There are many reasons why we might not feel good about ourselves on a fundamental level. I am reminded here of Larkin's poem 'This be the verse':

This be the verse
by Philip Larkin

They fuck you up, your mum and dad
They may not mean to, but they do.
They fill you with the faults they had
And add some extra, just for you.

But they were fucked up in their turn
By fools in old-style hats and coats,
Who half the time were soppy-stern
And half at one another's throats.

Man hands on misery to man.
It deepens like a coastal shelf.
Get out as early as you can,
And don't have any kids yourself.[21]

Larkin's solution to the problem does not seem to me to be all that useful, and in fact I feel that having children can be useful to us in this respect. My own experience of having a son gave me a new perspective on my own parents. I had this deep sense of unconditional love for my son, which I knew I would, however, fail to realize fully. The fact that, in the day-to-day life of having children, we are bound often not to be able to keep in touch with this sense of unconditional love, though we know it is there somewhere, makes me believe that it was there for my own parents as well. Indeed, I think it is there for nearly all parents, even though none of us is able to fully actualize it.

Whatever the reasons why we lack a basic sense of love and care for ourselves, we need to find ways of developing a more positive attitude towards ourselves if we are going to fully turn towards our own experience. The attitude we need is one of genuine interest in how we are. I have already mentioned the idea of care, and it is interesting to note that care appears in Roman mythology. Cura, Latin for 'care', is associated with the creation of the human being as shown in the following story:

> Cura, crossing a river, gathers clay from the riverbed
> and, deep in thought, moulds it into two figures, as she
> contemplates her creation. Jove appears, and Cura petitions
> the god to grant life to what she has made. Jove grants
> 'breath' to the clay figures, which come alive. Cura then
> asks the god if she can give them her name, but Jove will
> not allow this, feeling that, as it was he who gave them
> breath, they should be known after himself. While these
> two dispute, Tellos, Earth, appears and lays claim to the
> creations, as they are made from her body. The three
> failing to agree call upon Saturn, renowned for his wisdom
> in judging a dispute. He determines that Jove having
> granted life should receive the spirit at death, while Tellos
> should take back the body to herself. To Cura he grants the
> 'care' of them during life. He then rules that they should be
> known as 'homo', 'human being', because they were made
> from humus, earth.

Heidegger refers to this fable when he adopts the concept of care as central to his understanding of what allows 'being' to find authenticity in the world. Also, he notes the double meaning of care as we noted in respect to the William Carlos Williams poem, of having cares and taking care. It is perhaps this double meaning that gives the word its power, as the meanings are related in a very important way. As we have stressed, turning towards means taking care of what we tend to want to turn away from, that is turning towards our suffering as well as the suffering of others and the world. But our ability to do this depends on us being rooted in love, having a foundation of self-kindness and care.

Chapter nine

....

Our own aliveness in life itself

This foundation should not be confused with self-obsession, which seems to be promoted as the road to happiness in our modern world. It is not a narcissistic state, but rather one that is based on being in a real feeling relationship with the world. We would do well to remind ourselves of another myth here:

> In Greek mythology, Echo was a wood nymph who loved a youth by the name of Narcissus. He was a beautiful creature loved by many, but Narcissus loved no one. He enjoyed attention, praise and envy. In Narcissus' eyes, nobody matched him and as such he considered none were worthy of him.
>
> Echo's passion for Narcissus was equaled only by her passion for talking as she always had to have the last word. One day she enabled the escape of the goddess Juno's adulterous husband by engaging Juno in conversation. On finding out Echo's treachery, Juno cursed Echo by removing her voice with the exception that she could only speak that which was spoken to her.
>
> Echo often waited in the woods to see Narcissus, hoping for a chance to be noticed. One day as she lingered in the bushes he heard her footsteps and called out 'Who's here?' Echo replied 'Here!' Narcissus called again 'Come', Echo replied 'Come!' Narcissus called once more 'Why do you shun me?... Let us join one another.' Echo was overjoyed that Narcissus had asked her to join him. She longed to tell him who she was and of all the love she had for him in her heart, but she could not speak. She ran towards him and threw herself upon him.
>
> Narcissus became angry 'Hands off! I would rather die than you should have me!' and threw Echo to the

....

ground. Echo left the woods, her heart broken. Ashamed she ran away to live in the mountains yearning for a love that would never be returned. The grief killed her. Her body became one with the mountain stone. All that remained was her voice which replied in kind when others spoke.

Narcissus continued to attract many nymphs all of whom he briefly entertained, before refusing them. The gods grew tired of his behaviour and cursed Narcissus. They wanted him to know what it felt like to love and never be loved. They made it so there was only one whom he would love, someone who was not real and could never love him back.

One day whilst out enjoying the sunshine Narcissus came upon a pool of water. As he gazed into it, he caught a glimpse of what he thought was a beautiful water spirit. He did not recognise his own reflection and was immediately enamoured. Narcissus bent down his head to kiss the vision. As he did so the reflection mimicked his actions. Taking this as a sign of reciprocation Narcissus reached into the pool to draw the water spirit to him. The water displaced and the vision was gone. He panicked, where had his love gone? When the water became calm the water spirit returned. 'Why, beautiful being, do you shun me? Surely my face is not one to repel you. The nymphs love me, and you yourself look not indifferent upon me. When I stretch forth my arms you do the same, and you smile upon me and answer my beckoning with the like.' Again he reached out and again his love disappeared. Frightened to touch the water Narcissus lay still by the pool gazing into the eyes of his vision.

He cried in frustration. As he did so Echo also cried. He did not move, he did not eat or drink, he only suffered. He became gaunt, losing his beauty. The nymphs that loved him pleaded with him to come away from the pool. As they did so Echo also pleaded with him. He was transfixed; he wanted to stay there forever. Narcissus, like Echo, died with grief. His body

The Myth of Meditation

disappeared and where his body once lay a flower grew in its place. The nymphs mourned his death and as they mourned Echo also mourned.[22]

The myth has many variations, but they all act as a caution against self-absorption and taking the surface impression of things, in this case the reflection in the pool, as the truth of things. When our sense of self-worth is based on the superficial, we are bound at some point to suffer, perhaps not the literal fate of Narcissus, but a collapse of our sense of worth. I increasingly feel that where we have to find our sense of self-care is within our relationship with the world, and in particular in feeling into the resonance of our own aliveness with life itself: it is in this resonance that we can build a deep care for ourselves and the world.

Here then is a meditation that explores this resonance.

 ## Energy-circuits meditation

Take your time to set up the posture, making sure that you are as comfortable as possible and aligned. Try and have a sense of your skull in relation to your pelvis, and feel into the length of your back, right up to the crown of your head. Imagine and remember the earth below you and the sky above you. Give yourself time to settle. When you feel ready, begin to notice your breath: bring awareness to how you are drawing it in from outside, from the world around you.

Staying aware of your breath, take your attention to the soles of your feet. Begin to imagine that you are breathing through the soles of your feet, as if there were a second kind of more subtle breath that was linked to your normal breathing. So breathing in, draw the breath into the feet, and, breathing out, imagine the breath leaving through the soles. As you do this, try and have a sense of letting go of any holding on in your feet. Over the next few minutes, taking your time, slowly let your attention move into every part of your feet and then into the lower legs. This needs to be linked to your actual breath. As you breathe in, become increasingly involved with the feelings in your feet and legs, and, as you breathe out, let go of any tension you find there. Move up the legs through the knees and into the big muscles and bones of the upper legs, then into the buttocks and the pelvic floor. End up drawing the breath from the feet right up to the 'hara' – just below the navel, in the centre of the body rather than on the surface. We are imagining drawing in energy from the earth through the feet up to the hara, and then on the out-breath releasing down from the hara through the legs and out of the feet. Do not try and force anything in particular to happen: try and have a sense of playfulness, and do not get caught up in worrying about whether it is 'working' or not. We are using the imagination to support a coming into the lower body – we do not have to take it too seriously. Enjoy!

When you have done this for five minutes or so, do the same thing starting with the hands. Bring attention to the hands with the in-breath, and release on the out-breath. This time we are going to move slowly through the hands into the lower arms and so on, ending up drawing all the way to the heart centre. When you have done this, bring back the feeling of drawing up from the feet. See if you can have a sense of drawing in to the hara and the heart at the same time. Again try and do this in a light way, not forcing or worrying about doing it right.

We are going to add one more energy circuit: the central channel. This can be imagined from the root or base to the crown of the head, running just in front of your spine. Start from the base, your perineum between your anus and sexual organs, and slowly draw up the energy on the in-breath. Take your time to move through the lower body into the chest and right up to the crown. Again no forcing, just a light imagining. Be interested in what it feels like: it might be that you also start to feel that you are drawing energy down through the crown as you draw up, the two streams of energy meeting around the heart, or it might be just coming up from the earth. Notice what it feels like rather than trying to impose an idea on your experience.

Once you have established some sense of the central channel, add the other two secondary circuits back in: the feet and the hands. These feed into the central channel, so you have all three going at once. Do this for a while, until you have had enough, then just relax. Keeping the posture, stop trying to do anything and just sit with your natural breath for a little longer.

This might all sound rather complicated but it's really not. See it as a way of paying attention to the energy of the body. We are, as I have been emphasizing, not trying to force anything. It is light and playful and you cannot do it wrong: it is just a way of bringing a slightly different awareness into the body, and sensing into the body's natural aliveness and relationship to the external world.

What I have outlined above is just one way of going about trying to sense into the energetic aspects of our experience. You do not necessarily have to do it in the way I have suggested, or while you are doing it you might find another way of approaching the practice. I think in general, whatever tack you take, you do need to involve your breath. The breath is really the key to sensing into your body: it keeps the meditation rooted in sensations rather than it all becoming an idea. When we do this sort of thing we are using the imagination, but this is different from thinking in that we are not just overlaying our actual direct experience with an idea; rather, we are trying to support our experience with our imagination. One way of understanding this is that we are using an image. In the case above, the image is of drawing in energy from the world around us, up from the earth and down from the sky, and opening our bodies to this energy. It is much more a feeling than an intellectual idea, so we need to keep the whole thing quite light rather than trying to force something to happen. Also, we need to be open to our imagination taking us in a different direction. If it does, feel free to go with it; this is, as I have said, different from just imposing some intellectual idea upon our experience. The imagination is quite delicate and cannot be forced: it kicks in when we relax and pay attention to what is happening in our bodies.

With the above meditation, we are trying to get an energetic sense of our own bodies, trying to experience them as full of life. When we manage to do this, we start to feel a stronger connection to the world, as the world is full of life and this life, the life of the world, is the same life as in our own bodies. Here is a poem that speaks to this basic relationship between all life:

Hokusai says
by Roger Keyes

Hokusai says look carefully.
He says pay attention, notice.

He says keep looking, stay curious.
He says there is no end to seeing

He says look forward to getting old.
He says keep changing,
you just get more who you really are.
He says get stuck, accept it, repeat
yourself as long as it is interesting.

He says keep doing what you love.

He says keep praying.

He says every one of us is a child,
every one of us is ancient
every one of us has a body.
He says every one of us is frightened.
He says every one of us has to find
a way to live with fear.

He says everything is alive –
shells, buildings, people, fish,
mountains, trees, wood is alive.
Water is alive.

Everything has its own life.

Everything lives inside us.

He says live with the world inside you.

He says it doesn't matter if you draw,
or write books. It doesn't matter
if you saw wood, or catch fish.
It doesn't matter if you sit at home
and stare at the ants on your veranda
or the shadows of the trees
and grasses in your garden.
It matters that you care.

It matters that you feel.
It matters that you notice.
It matters that life lives through you.

Contentment is life living through you.
Joy is life living through you.
Satisfaction and strength
is life living through you.

He says don't be afraid.
Don't be afraid.

Love, feel, let life take you by the hand.

Let life live through you.[23]

I find the idea expressed in this poem, of life living through you, very helpful. It seems to me to capture a way of being in the world that supports us to find our essential nature. The poem also suggests that this attitude comes about through paying attention. It is interesting that the words are put in the mouth of the artist Hokusai. Best known in the West for his views of Mount Fuji and the 'The great wave off Kanagawa', he produced a great many drawings and prints, but most of the best were done in old age. He writes in the postscript of *One Hundred Views of Mount Fuji*:

> From the age of six, I had the habit of sketching from life.
> I became an artist and from fifty on began making works
> that won some reputation, but nothing I did before the
> age of seventy was worthy of attention. At seventy-three,
> I began to grasp the structure of birds and beasts, insects
> and fish and of the way plants grew. If I go on trying I
> will surely understand them still better by the time I am
> eighty-six, so that by ninety I will have penetrated to
> their essential nature. At one hundred, I may well have
> a positively divine understanding of them, while at one
> hundred and thirty, forty, or more I will have reached
> the stage where every dot and every stroke I paint will
> be alive. May Heaven, that grants long life, give me the
> chance to prove that this is no lie.[24]

I like these words from Hokusai: they seem to me to reflect a sense of 'calling', of giving one's life to something one cares for, and of taking care. I find in them an attitude that is close to the one needed for the meditator. As the poem says, 'there is no end to seeing', and it is the same for meditation. We do not get to an end – there is always more to uncover, we can always open more fully to the world.

It is important to understand that turning towards does not mean turning away from the world. We should not understand this image of turning towards as excluding anything at all. Often meditation is understood as a kind of extreme introversion, but this is not the case. We are not just turning towards what is 'inside' of us, and in particular we are not just turning towards our 'mental' experience: we are turning towards everything, everything in our experience, which includes our bodies and senses, along with our thoughts and feelings. This is expressed in the poem by the line 'He says live with the world inside you.'

As with all images, turning towards has its limitations; in this case, to turn towards implies that we also turn away from something else, so to clarify we need another image as well. Abiding or opening is another way of understanding what we are trying to do. This has the advantage of not implying a turning away. However, I am using turning towards as it is very hard, at least to start with, to just sit in a completely open state. Before we can do this, we have to establish a firm foundation, through grounding, and we also have to uncover the areas of our experience that we have learned to habitually turn away from. So our ability to turn towards our full experience is dependent both on a general stability, found in the cultivation of the posture, and also on a basic sense of positive love for ourselves and the world that supports us. This sense of love begins with ourselves but is not based on feeling that we are somehow special, better than others; rather, it is based on a deep appreciation of ourselves as one way in which life expresses itself. We are trying to develop a sense of intimacy with ourselves that is not dependent upon the love of others or the esteem we are held in by others. Here is another poem by Derek Walcott:

Love after love
by Derek Walcott

The time will come
when, with elation
you will greet yourself arriving
at your own door, in your own mirror
and each will smile at the other's welcome,

and say, sit here. Eat.
You will love again the stranger who was your self.
Give wine. Give bread. Give back your heart
to itself, to the stranger who has loved you

all your life, whom you ignored
for another, who knows you by heart.
Take down the love letters from the bookshelf,

the photographs, the desperate notes,
peel your own image from the mirror.
Sit. Feast on your life.[25]

Walcott touches here upon a basic loss of intimacy with ourselves, the loss of a sense that we are inherently of worth, and that this worth does not have to depend upon others but can be found within ourselves. For many of us, regaining this kind of love for ourselves will take time and a patient, consistent effort. However, it is an interesting and worthwhile journey, and one in which meditation can play an important part. One of the main problems that many of us face is an unrealistic idea of how we 'should' be, by which I mean that many people feel that they need to be perfect and, when they do not match up to these internalized ideals, which of course we never can, they are left with a feeling of failure and defeat. It is all too easy to bring these kinds of ideals into 'spiritual' practice. When we do this, practice no longer supports us but becomes just another way to feel bad about ourselves, another way to beat ourselves up.

Within Japanese art, we find the idea of wabi-sabi as a central characteristic. Although difficult to translate, it is based on the ideas that nothing lasts, nothing is finished, and nothing is perfect. These three characteristics are taken from Buddhism, being related to the 'three marks' of reality. So, in trying to capture reality, Japanese art values these characteristics as giving beauty and authenticity. It is quite different from the Western ideal of perfection in art, the influence of which spreads beyond art to a feeling for life itself. I think wabi-sabi is one way of expressing a very vital understanding: beauty and authenticity are not to be found in perfection, which is an abstract notion that does not in reality exist; rather, it is to be found in the very imperfection that is the true nature of reality. When we let go of the ego fantasy of being 'perfect' and begin to look carefully at who we really are, we begin to find in our very imperfection a depth and beauty that is missed when we are constantly burdened with some abstract ideal of perfection.

The language of spiritual practice is very often peppered with words like 'enlightenment', 'perfection', and so on. When we take on this language in a naive way, we set ourselves up for a fall: our practice becomes a means of confirming that we are never going to reach the 'goal'. One of the teachings central to Buddhism is that of understanding all of its teachings as a raft, something that helps us to make a difficult journey. Different teachings are useful to us at different times, but none of them should become a burden – we do not have to carry the raft on our backs after it has served its purpose. Of course this analogy of a person carrying a raft around on his or her back after it has carried them over the dangerous water also has its limitations, as it implies that there is a place of absolute safety, a place where everything has been finally resolved. This too should not be taken on literally. In the end, life is what it is; we have a life and try to make the most we can of it. Any idea of some kind of absolute redemption or perfection is, I think, just another ego fantasy. I am reminded of some words of Raymond Carver:

The Myth of Meditation

Late fragment
by Raymond Carver

And did you get what
you wanted from this life, even so?
I did.
And what did you want?
To call myself beloved, to feel myself
beloved on the earth.[26]

I find these few words very moving, partly because they seem to acknowledge the transitory nature of life, and because they locate the meaning of life in life itself. This seems to me to be in contrast to so much of what we find in 'religion', which often strikes me as anti-life, rejecting life, turning away from the wabi-sabi of it all.

So we have this image of turning towards, a turning towards what is there in our experience. It is related to taking care, and it is in and of itself an act of love. In the act of abiding with ourselves as we are, we are confirming our own basic worth; we are gradually allowing our 'mind' to reveal itself more and more fully to itself. This process of uncovering can only happen when we are not trying to push our experience in a particular direction.

It is confusing that, on the one hand, we have these practices within Buddhism that seem to be quite explicitly trying to direct the mind in a particular direction, towards awareness or love, while on the other hand there also seems to be this need just to be with our experience as it is. There seems to be this contradiction between the active and the receptive, or we might even term it the masculine and the feminine aspect. And to some degree this is the case. At times we will want to be more active, to intervene in order to bring about a desired result. This is not a problem, or at least it is not a problem as long as it is part of a balanced approach that still allows for an open, less structured sitting. I feel that it is always a good thing to leave a little time after doing any practice just to sit. This allows you both to absorb the practice and also to let go of any straining to attain a particular result.

In the following meditation, taken from one of my earlier books, *The Body*,[27] I have tried to bring together the receptive and active elements of practice in a version of the loving-kindness meditation, or Mettā Bhāvanā.

 ## The Mettā Bhāvanā using the body and the breath

Sitting in your meditation posture, take the time you need to get comfortable and let the body settle.

Begin by listening to the world around you: let whatever sounds there are remind you that you are in the world, and that this practice is within the context of the world and for the world as well as yourself. Do not strain to hear – just notice whatever sounds there are, notice how these sounds naturally arise in your awareness and fall away. As you listen in a relaxed way, let your face begin to soften. Notice how your face feels. Imagine your face letting go around the eyes and the jaw. Notice what your face feels like as if you are 'listening' to your face. Your face is what you show to the world, and often we feel obliged to put on a brave face for the world; see if you can let your face just express your heart. Breathe your face, letting it soften on your out-breath. Feel how sensitive your face is, how it holds your character and history. Let your face speak to you.

From the face, move through the rest of your body, using your breath to support the awareness as you slowly move it through your body. Use your imagination; for instance, imagine your spine, alive, made up not just of bone but of soft tissue, nerves, and fluids. Breathe into the different areas of your body; for example, breathing in, be aware of the pelvis, and, breathing out, be aware of the pelvis. If any images of particular feelings, emotions, or thoughts related to this kind of listening to your body arise, be aware of them. Try not to elaborate on them with the rational mind – just let the image or feeling be there naturally until it fades away. As you become aware of different areas of your body, encourage a sense of appreciation for them, recognizing how they enrich your life in a basic and fundamental way. I find the hands particularly good in this respect.

If there are parts of your body that feel numb, breathe into them a warm kind breath. Do not force them to respond; just listen to them and be open to what arises. Take your time, seeing this as an act of mettā or loving-kindness towards your body. Pay particular attention to your belly and the area around your heart. Try and approach all of this in a receptive way, as if you are letting your body say what it wants to say, rather than you trying to force awareness into it or demanding a response. Do not interrogate the body, but abide with it and let it sing its songs. The body might speak to us directly, through sensations, but also through images. Perhaps your hands feel like birds, your belly like an oven, your heart like a stone – be sensitive to the language your body uses, accept the image or the thought, however outlandish it might be. If you do find images arising, try not to interpret them, but let the image speak to you directly.

When you feel ready, introduce the idea of mettā with a simple phrase that resonates with you; see if you can let it come to you as if from the heart. Imagine your heart speaking directly: use your breath to open up a sense of space around your heart and listen to the longing that enters that space. If nothing comes, suggest a phrase to your heart: 'May I care deeply for myself', 'May I love myself as I am in this moment.' Watch and listen to your body – imagine what mettā feels like in your body. Most importantly, treat yourself with kindness.

After we have established a sense of loving-kindness in our own bodies, we can move through the other stages of the practice. The next being feeling mettā towards a close friend, the third towards what is often called a neutral person, so someone we have no strong feelings towards, then fourthly towards an enemy, and lastly towards all living beings. So we will see here that we have moved through the full range of our hearts, ending with the sense of just opening up completely to the world.

In the other stages of the meditation, try to keep a sense of your body. One thing that I often do is just imagine the person that I think of breathing as I breathe. So the breath becomes a link. As you breathe in, think of your friend breathing in; as you breathe out, think of your friend breathing out. Imagine the breath opening their heart as it opens yours; imagine the breath bringing life into their body as it brings life into your body. In this way, we keep the practice simple and direct, and we encourage the feeling of interconnection – an awareness of the life force that we share with all beings. Let go of any idea of having to 'produce' mettā and pump it out: be content to just 'breathe with'. Try doing the same with the other stages, placing an emphasis on what it feels like rather than having to make something happen.

There is no one 'right' way of doing this practice. I feel that it is better to understand it in terms of an enquiry into your own heart, rather than seeing it as an exercise where you manufacture 'love' and then send it out into the world to help others. This seems to me to be a little bit too much for most of us, and even has the danger of making us feel as if we are in some sense better than those poor people who are so in need of our mettā.

The rather paradoxical aspect of practising the Mettā Bhāvanā, which is after all meant to be concerned with our emotions, is that in many people it provokes overthinking. So we should try not to get too complicated, avoid making up stories, and just keep to very simple direct thoughts, all the time staying aware of the body, particularly around the heart and the belly.

In this practice, we are looking for a balance between being receptive and being active when we sit. At other times, we can just sit with the breath in a very simple way, just doing nothing at all other than using the natural breath to provide a bit of an anchor. And we also pay some attention to the posture, which I hope by now we understand as intimately conjoined to the breath. So when we just sit in this way, we are not clinging to our breath for dear life, we are not trying to get concentrated or absorbed – we are just abiding with ourselves, noticing with care the way experience unfolds in our awareness. I will talk a little more about this under the heading of 'seeing through'.

Chapter ten

···

Beings thrown into time and history

Turning towards is not something that we do just in meditation; indeed all of meditation is really something that we are doing in the hope that it will overspill into our lives in a more general sense. Most of our opportunities to turn towards are going to occur in our everyday lives. Meditation is then to be understood as a means of sensitizing ourselves to daily life, which we so often go through in a barely aware state. So in meditation we have an opportunity to develop qualities that we want to bring into the rest of our lives. We are doing a formal training to strengthen our ability to be more aware and loving in the rest of our lives. I often find myself telling people that meditation is no substitute, or compensation, for life. Only when we begin to 'remember' to be aware and kind outside of our meditation can we say that meditation is starting to really work.

Extending turning towards into our everyday lives means just noticing all those times when we feel an impulse to turn away, and, on noticing this turning away, just trying to experience it as fully as possible. As we have already noted, this turning away might sometimes be quite extreme. Feelings of shame are a good example of this: those times when we wish the earth would open up, as they say. Such feelings are often associated with strong physical experience, such as blushing or a feeling of sinking in the belly and so on; this means they are easy to recognize, if hard to stay with. But much of our turning away is far more subtle and not so easy to recognize: it often manifests as thoughts. It is all those times when the ego feels threatened in some way or other, those times when we are defensive or aggressive because something has happened that undermines our sense of ourselves in one way or another. These times are very valuable to us.

Just as we are trying to bring meditation into daily life, we are also interested in bringing daily life into meditation. By this I mean we can use meditation as a space in which we can explore those things that happen to us in life that leave a kind of stain on our minds.

For example, I have from boyhood suffered from very poor sight. This meant as a child I had to wear glasses with thick lenses, which was a source of embarrassment and even shame for me. I would feel quite intense feelings of shame whenever my poor sight was alluded to by others. Later as a meditator I found that these feelings would come into awareness and I would react to them in the same way. I would feel I wanted to get away from them; I would feel myself turning away, perhaps clutching at the practice to try and make them go. In time, I learned to stay with them. Staying with in this sense means just staying with the feelings rather than going into some rationalization around them. Just accepting the feelings, breathing with them. In time, when we do this we will find that they are released, but for this to happen we have to be prepared to feel them fully. We cannot think ourselves out of them, but we can abide with them in a kind way – and it is this kind of abiding that makes meditation such a wonderful and effective practice. It does, however, take time.

So turning towards or abiding is our basic method, which is carried out on the foundation of grounding. It is psychological in the sense that it is concerned with the psyche, but it is not psychological in the sense of being concerned with trying to figure out, think through, or analyze ourselves. Within meditation, turning towards is receptive rather than active in relationship to the ego. Although we might employ certain forms of practice such as Mindfulness of Breathing or Mettā Bhāvanā to engage the imagination, we employ these in a conscious but light way, never letting them become an overlay to our felt experience, not using them to mask what is there.

Our psyche is in its deep nature polytheistic; to not understand this is to be forever trying to impose upon it a fantasy of the ego.

The fantasy of the 'spiritually' aspiring ego is one of purification or transcendence. It is ironically a fantasy of destruction of the ego. In turning towards, we are not trying to destroy anything or transcend anything; rather, we are attempting to let everything have its place, to find a place, in our psyche, where the diverse and sometimes contradictory aspects of ourselves can co-exist. Often, when we begin a practice like meditation, we see it in terms of resolving conflicts and moving towards a unification of the psyche; while this can serve us to some degree, as a model it should not be taken at face value. I am here reminded of the myth of Persephone – as with all myths, it has many variations, but the essentials of the myth are given below.

Demeter, goddess of fruitfulness and harvest, has one daughter, Persephone, the maiden of spring. Zeus, her father, promises her to his brother Hades, god of the underworld, who has fallen in love with her. One day, when Persephone is picking flowers, the ground opens up and Hades appears in his chariot pulled by jet-black horses, kidnaps Persephone, and brings her down to be his wife in the underworld. Grief-stricken and confused, Demeter withholds her gifts from the world, without which it will become a wasteland. She comes down to earth to search for her daughter. The sun god Helios tells her that Persephone has been taken to the underworld by Hades; Demeter threatens to allow the earth to wither and never to return to Olympus unless her daughter is restored to her. Finally, Zeus intervenes by telling Hermes to go down to the underworld and bring Persephone back. Hades knows he must agree to Zeus' terms, but he gives Persephone a pomegranate seed, knowing that, if she eats it, she will have to return to him. With her daughter back, Demeter rejoins the other gods on Mount Olympus. But, because Persephone does eat the pomegranate seed, she must return to the underworld for four months a year. In these months, Demeter grieves and the earth goes through winter.

In this myth, the conflict is resolved, but not completely to any of the participants' satisfaction; there is a compromise: Hades must have his due. I think this is important. We have a fantasy about resolution in the absolute or the light, but the underworld cannot be ignored. Winter gives contrast and meaning to summer. Often the spiritual fantasy is one in which all psychological complexes are resolved, either in life through 'enlightenment' where the 'dark' is fully dispelled, or in the next world through unification with the father. However, the psyche gets its energy from its complexes; it is in its nature complex. Such a resolution, even if possible, would result in an inert state.

Historically and mythologically, Buddhism recognizes this problem and attempts to overcome it with the elevation of the bodhisattva ideal, replacing that of the arhant. Here the final enlightenment, which is a 'blowing out', is put off in order for the aspirant to help all other beings to enlightenment. Hence compassion is given equal weight to wisdom; the arhant striving for individual liberation is replaced by the altruism of the bodhisattva whose practice is now the liberation of all beings. This task is of course impossible, and in addition has the problem of tending towards a kind of abstraction, as we can read in the following myth.

Avalokiteśvara has made a vow to put off his own enlightenment until he has liberated all beings from suffering. To this end, he works tirelessly for countless ages, then, looking down on the earth, he sees that all his great efforts have made little difference: there are still innumerable beings suffering. On seeing this, he is greatly moved and begins to weep. His tears form a lake out of which a lotus rises with Green Tārā seated upon it.

We might understand his tears as those of compassion, but we might also understand them as those of despair. This interpretation is strengthened by another myth where, instead of weeping, he literally explodes and is reconstituted as eleven-headed and thousand-armed. We might understand his multiple heads not only as allowing him to see everywhere, but also as offering the possibility of different perspectives on what he sees.

We should also note that his name means 'Lord who looks down'. Here there is implied a certain separation: he is above looking down on suffering humanity. In contrast, Tārā steps down into the world, lives in the world. This is why she is perhaps the most popular of Buddhist archetypes in many parts of the Buddhist world. So one way of reading this myth is to see that the lofty ideal of the bodhisattva tends towards a separation from the earth, or indeed an abstraction into the theoretical, a rising above the concerns of the psyche. There has to be a coming back to earth, and this is achieved through despair or a breakdown. Out of this comes a compassion that is responsive to what is directly felt rather than seen from above. Interestingly, one form of Tārā is the seven-eyed, where she has eyes both in the palms of her hands and the soles of her feet, along with the third eye of wisdom in her brow.

But it might be that the 'descent' of the bodhisattva to earth in the form of Tārā is still not enough, and, as our previous story implies, the journey must go further or deeper, into the underworld.

With all these stories, we are not concerned with giving them a definite or fixed interpretation – it is important that they remain fluid, able to shift meaning as our own perspective changes. Their meaning is always contingent on where they are viewed from. This is of vital importance when we turn towards: what we 'see' is constantly liable to change.We should not be trying to come to any definitive resolution of our experience, but understand it, as with the 'soul', as fathomless and always capable of being researched, seen again in another way. When we understand practice as research, we understand, as Hokusai says, that we should 'keep looking', that 'there is no end to seeing'.

Meditation has only a partial part to play in the process that we are considering here, by which I mean the role of meditation is to provide a space in which the mind can research itself. This type of research or enquiry will need to be supported by other activities that nourish and sustain the soul in its unfolding. This may include any of the arts and also the employment of the intellect through reading and study. It can be tempting to reject the intellect, even to regard it as a hindrance to the soul. I have repeatedly stressed that in meditation we are not trying to think through our experience; this is because within meditation we are trying to give room to other aspects of our awareness. I do not, however, wish to imply that outside of meditation itself the intellect is unimportant. My own understanding of meditation has been formed not only through practice of meditation but also through ideas found in philosophy and psychology, and perhaps most importantly, in my case, poetry. We have experiences when we meditate, but these experiences do not come ready-made with meaning: their meaning for us will depend on our understanding them in other ways.

This is important because it is not uncommon, when people get involved in spiritual practice, for them to feel that they need nothing else; they sometimes even feel that they no longer need other people, they no longer need to be in relationship with others and the world – it is all too mundane for them. Compared to the wonderful experience they may have in practice, everything else is trivial. We find this kind of attitude in many traditions, as if turning your face to God is to turn away from life, but this is not our interest here. We are historical, psychological beings, and it is as beings thrown into time and history that we are interested. The turning towards ourselves is not a turning away from the world. Here is a poem that played a pivotal part in my adoption of the idea of 'turning towards' as one of the central themes in this book:

Musée des beaux arts
by W.H. Auden

About suffering they were never wrong,
The Old Masters: how well they understood
Its human position; how it takes place
While someone else is eating or opening a window or just
    walking dully along;
How, when the aged are reverently, passionately waiting
For the miraculous birth, there always must be
Children who did not specially want it to happen, skating
On a pond at the edge of the wood:
They never forgot
That even the dreadful martyrdom must run its course
Anyhow in a corner, some untidy spot
Where the dogs go on with their doggy life and the
    torturer's horse
Scratches its innocent behind on a tree.

The Myth of Meditation

In Brueghel's Icarus, for instance: how everything turns
    away
Quite leisurely from the disaster; the plowman may
Have heard the splash, the forsaken cry,
But for him it was not an important failure; the sun shone
As it had to on the white legs disappearing into the green
Water; and the expensive delicate ship that must have seen
Something amazing, a boy falling out of the sky,
Had somewhere to get to and sailed calmly on.[28]

This is a very rich poem in terms of image. It will not be hard to see why it struck me when I came across it, and this was reinforced by knowing, quite well, the picture that Auden refers to in the poem. I think that this poem and the painting are very good examples of how the arts can offer us a degree of insight into ourselves.

One of the questions that Auden's poem raises for me is this: what is the relationship between our turning towards ourselves and our turning towards the world? I am not going to address this question directly, but I think it will be clear from what I have already said that, for me, the two kinds of turning towards are closely related. I hope that, if this is not already clear, it will become so as we turn towards the last of our three main topics, seeing through. But before we do, I want to introduce another practice that offers a kind of bridge between turning towards and seeing through, as well as addressing the issue of the relationship between individual suffering and universal suffering, which is at the very heart of our practice. This practice is mainly found in the Tibetan Buddhist tradition. It is known as 'tonglen', which means something like 'receiving and giving'. I will give the traditional form of this meditation, but you can of course find your own way of using the basic principles in your practice.

Tonglen meditation

The practice is linked to the breath. We imagine breathing in the suffering of others, sometimes in the form of dark smoke. So we breathe in, aware of the suffering around us. We take this down deep in the body to the belly, and then, on the out-breath, we imagine breathing out love. So we are using our own body to purify the suffering of others.

We might do this in a general sort of way, or we might imagine a particular kind of suffering, for example, anger.

While this practice is often done as a formal sitting practice, it might also be done in our daily life. If we encounter suffering in the world, instead of turning away from it we deliberately breathe it in. However, I think perhaps the most practical and effective use of this practice is to employ it whenever we feel ourselves in the grip of some difficult emotion. In this version, when we feel anger, we bring to mind that there are countless other people who at the same moment are suffering from this same emotion; many are perhaps experiencing it in a much more distressing way than we are. So we imagine breathing in their anger and breathing out kindness towards them. We can do this at any time. For instance, you feel yourself getting frustrated at the supermarket: you are in a rush, and someone in front of you in the queue is taking forever to pay for their groceries. You feel the frustration rising in you, and then you begin to breathe in a conscious way, thinking of all those people who are suffering far more from frustration than you are, people who every day have to queue for hours to get a loaf of bread or even for water. So you imagine breathing in these far more serious frustrations, and breathing out calm and love. Here is a poem that suggests the power of acknowledging the suffering of others, and the possible transformative effects of such an acknowledgement when it is done with sufficient depth of feeling:

The Myth of Meditation

Kindness
by Naomi Shihab Nye

Before you know what kindness really is
you must lose things,
feel the future dissolve in a moment
like salt in a weakened broth.
What you held in your hand,
what you counted and carefully saved,
all this must go so you know
how desolate the landscape can be
between the regions of kindness.
How you ride and ride
thinking the bus will never stop,
the passengers eating maize and chicken
will stare out the window forever.

Before you learn the tender gravity of kindness,
you must travel where the Indian in a white poncho
lies dead by the side of the road.
You must see how this could be you,
how he too was someone
who journeyed through the night with plans
and the simple breath that kept him alive.

Before you know kindness as the deepest thing inside,
you must know sorrow as the other deepest thing.
You must wake up with sorrow.
You must speak to it till your voice
catches the thread of all sorrows
and you see the size of the cloth.

Then it is only kindness that makes sense anymore,
only kindness that ties your shoes
and sends you out into the day to mail letters and purchase
      bread,
only kindness that raises its head
from the crowd of the world to say
It is I you have been looking for,
and then goes with you everywhere
like a shadow or a friend.[29]

I hope this does not all sound too stark and depressing. I am aware that there is a lot of suffering being talked about here, and yet the people I know who, rather than going through life trying to pretend that suffering is not there, or that it does not touch them, instead practise in a way that confronts suffering are usually full of good humour. I hope I myself fit into this picture. I think that one of the things that develops through practice is a kind of robust good humour. It is important not to take it all too seriously in a dour kind of way: there needs to be joy and light along with the willingness to be 'real'.

When I worked as a volunteer in a hospice, which I did for five years in San Francisco, I was often struck by how positive people were when they faced death. Of course this was not always the case, but it was not uncommon. This was all the more striking as it was an AIDS hospice, so the majority of those who came to us to die were relatively young men. I have also had a number of good friends who have had to face terminal illnesses relatively young, and who faced their fate with astonishing positivity. Reflecting on this, it seems to me that, when we finally take on our death, the fear of it dissipates. It is as if the constant attempt to hold it off, to keep it at arm's length, is what causes us much of our distress in life.

Buddhism stresses coming into relationship with our own mortality, as does existentialism in the Western tradition. Both do this because they share the insight that our turning away from the reality of death means that we can never live a full and authentic life. We are in an existential sense living a lie. The preciousness of human life can only be fully appreciated in relation to its finite nature. An acceptance of death means that we are inclined to make the most of our lives. Death is such a fearful event only in so far as we understand ourselves as self-existent, by which I mean we understand our own lives as something separate and distinct from the rest of life, rather than a particular temporal expression of life itself. I do not, however, wish to suggest that recognizing fully that we will die brings about instant joy; rather, it gives to life a certain positive gravitas, a certain weight that keeps us more fully in life, in the world. The word 'gravitas' is related to the word 'grave'; when we realize the fact of death, we find ourselves wanting to be meaningfully engaged with life.

Here is a short extract from a radio interview given by Dr Feelgood guitarist Wilko Johnson, where he talks about his experience just after learning about his terminal pancreatic cancer:

> We walked out of there and I felt an elation of spirit.
> You're walking along and suddenly you're vividly alive.
> You're looking at the trees and the sky and everything
> and it's just 'whoah'. I am actually a miserable person. I've
> spent most of my life moping in depressions and things,
> but this has all lifted.[30]

Part 3

Seeing through

Chapter eleven

....

The paradoxical aspect of seeing through

As I have already stated, the three parts in which I have organized this book should not be understood as either linear or self-contained. In the grounding, there is a turning towards and at least the intimation of 'seeing through'. The turning towards necessitates a grounding and sets up the conditions for seeing through.

Seeing through itself has the suggestion of both a seeing through *of* and a seeing through *to*. In a basic sense, we can say we see through our normal mode of consciousness: we understand it from a different perspective. So we see through to another way of understanding and being in the world. Here is one of my favourite poems; it is, as much of Stevens' work, kind of opaque, suggestive, and somewhat mysterious. I think it can be read as a meditation or a reflection. For me, it seems to open up the possibility of multiple ways of understanding the world and of being free from a fixed viewpoint that has come prior to experience itself.

Thirteen ways of looking at a blackbird
by Wallace Stevens

I
Among twenty snowy mountains,
The only moving thing
Was the eye of the blackbird.

II
I was of three minds,
Like a tree
In which there are three blackbirds.

III
The blackbird whirled in the autumn winds.
It was a small part of the pantomime.

IV
A man and a woman
Are one.
A man and a woman and a blackbird
Are one.

V
I do not know which to prefer,
The beauty of inflections
Or the beauty of innuendoes,
The blackbird whistling
Or just after.

VI
Icicles filled the long window
With barbaric glass.
The shadow of the blackbird
Crossed it, to and fro.
The mood
Traced in the shadow
An indecipherable cause.

VII
O thin men of Haddam,
Why do you imagine golden birds?
Do you not see how the blackbird
Walks around the feet
Of the women about you?

VIII
I know noble accents
And lucid, inescapable rhythms;
But I know, too,
That the blackbird is involved
In what I know.

IX
When the blackbird flew out of sight,
It marked the edge
Of one of many circles.

X
At the sight of blackbirds
Flying in a green light,
Even the bawds of euphony
Would cry out sharply.

XI
He rode over Connecticut
In a glass coach.
Once, a fear pierced him,
In that he mistook
The shadow of his equipage
For blackbirds.

XII
The river is moving.
The blackbird must be flying.

XIII
It was evening all afternoon.
It was snowing
And it was going to snow.
The blackbird sat
In the cedar-limbs.[31]

It is not that I really have much of an idea of what it is Stevens is trying to get at here, if indeed he is trying to get at anything – it is more just the mood of the whole thing. The 'blackbird', a common enough creature, is 'involved' in everything – love, fear, the rivers: the bird is involved in life and seems to become a motif for life itself.

We might tend to think that the idea of 'seeing through' is going to lead us to some kind of certainty and ultimate clarity about ourselves and life in general, but if we understand it in this way I think we will be let down by it. It is not an intellectual clarity about life, not a monotheistic certainty that is offered by this idea of seeing through. It is a kind of gnosis or knowing, but it is not one where everything becomes like an architectural drawing with precise clear lines, everything in its place and clearly demarcated from everything else. Sometimes there is a kind of clarity, a kind of light in which everything does become clear, but it is not graspable: it tends to dissolve as soon as we try to capture it, to pin it down. There is this opening up, or opening into, but once we try and 'understand' the experience from our normal perspective everything closes down again.

The 'mystic' traditions we find as substrata in all major faiths are not deliberately trying to 'mystify' – it is just that, when experience is viewed only from the narrow perspective of the intellect or the ego, it makes no 'real' sense. It is interesting that these mystic experiences are strikingly similar to one another even when they are underpinned by different theological understandings.

Anyway, we are getting a little ahead of ourselves, perhaps, and we should not think that 'seeing through' is necessarily going to be a 'mystic' experience, but it will have in common with such experience a quality that means it cannot be captured and held on to. The process by which we hold on to experience is a kind of calcification of fluid experience into hard facts or set stories. It is also often a simplification, a one-sided view. We had a 'happy' childhood or an 'unhappy' childhood; we were 'loved' or 'unloved' by our mother or father, and so on. If we keep telling ourselves the same stories, they take on the status of 'facts', 'histories'. But sometimes something happens, and here I mean in life, that shows us that there was more to it, that the idea we had of our mother, which was quite naturally an idea of 'mother', does not in *fact* adequately encompass that person at all. For when we fix our own experience, we also have to fix the other actors in the dramas of our life. So there is often a certain paradoxical aspect to seeing through: it will have a certain 'emotional' clarity, but it is also a willingness to abide with the complexity of our lives without our normal compulsion to understand in a reductive sense.

So it is a seeing through that can be understood as 'soul', which tends towards complexity and has an opaque quality. Nevertheless, this kind of seeing through may also well have a sense of letting go, or putting down something that has narrowed and limited our vision, our sense of ourselves and our ability to feel fully part of the world. This is quite difficult to understand as long as we view it from the perspective of the so-called rational mind, the mind of the modern age, the machine age, the computer age.

We can say that this kind of mind has the characteristic of literalism, which James Hillman has often talked about as allowing a word only one meaning, and then mistaking the word for the thing itself. Stevens, he of the blackbird, also has the line 'not an idea about the thing but the thing itself' in another of his poems, highlighting the same tendency to mistake our ideas for things, and therefore to impose on the thing our own characteristics. We might talk about this in terms of dualism, where there is no middle ground, everything is black or white. In addition, everything is me or other, I or not I. Here we can see that this problem is at the core of what Buddhism would call the belief in a fixed self or soul. There is a kind of rigidity that tries to make the world safe by attempting to separate it into sharply delineated parts. This is a problem because it is the imposition of an idea upon reality, an idea that will at some point break down, or if not break down will keep us from seeing and experiencing the richly complex world that we live in, along with the rich internal world of our own polytheistic psyches. It will tend to set us against the world, and our small self, that of the ego, against what we might call our big self.

Here is a traditional Buddhist practice that is aimed at beginning to loosen us up, to support us to realize that there is no sharp division between us and the world. It is a very rich practice that can take many years to fully explore. It can be understood and experienced on many levels, a few of which I will try to indicate. It is more than anything a practice that employs our imaginative faculty. It is based on the idea that the world can be understood as being composed of various elements. We find this idea in many cultures, although the elements might vary. This practice has its origins in the Indian Buddhist tradition and uses the elements of earth, water, fire, air, space, and consciousness. The basic idea behind this practice is to contemplate the six elements in turn, as they manifest both in ourselves and in the world outside of ourselves, and to realize that they are all empty of any unchanging essential nature and devoid of selfhood.

 ## The six-element practice

Once you have established your posture and taken the time you need to settle down and have a sense of being grounded, bring to mind the element earth. In this context, earth stands for everything that has solidity and density, has resistance and weight. We first contemplate this element as it makes up our own bodies. I normally start with the teeth, as they can be directly experienced, and go on to think about the bones and flesh, the nails and the hair, the organs of the body, and so on. We are contemplating and feeling into the earth element as it constitutes our own body. We can do this in an analytical and systematic kind of way if that appeals to us, or we can do it in a looser kind of way, just trying to have a feel for the element in us. We might also allow the emotional resonances of the element to come to mind. For instance, earth might seem to offer support and strength; it might also suggest density and a kind of heavy stuckness.

When we have established a sense of the element internally, we go on to imagine it as it manifests in the outside world. Here it stands for everything that has the qualities that we associate with earth, so will include rocks and trees, buildings, earth itself, other living beings, and so on – the list is more or less endless, so it is clearly more about getting a 'feel' for the element than having to cover everything that might be considered as earth.

When we have established a sense of earth externally, we then consider that the earth in us has come from the earth outside of us, by which I mean that the cells and the bones of our body have been built and maintained by taking in the element through eating. In addition, we consider that this element needs to be constantly maintained, and that we are also constantly losing the element from the body. We could say that the element moves through us like a slow river, being taken in from outside, being incorporated into us, and also passing through us. If we stopped taking in this element, we would not last very long. Then we bring to mind that one day we will die, and then this element will return to the element outside completely, and go on to make up other things in the world: there is no fixed or enduring self to be found anywhere in this element.

We then go through the other elements in the same way. We contemplate all the different fluids in the body under the element water, such as blood, tears, digestive juices, sweat, spinal fluid, and so on, and then all the various manifestations of water in the world's rivers, rain, dew, ice, and so on. Then we consider that this is the same element whether inside or outside of our bodies, and that we have to maintain this element as it makes us up by taking it in from outside, also encouraging the awareness that one day this element will return to the element outside, and that we cannot find any stable sense of self within this element.

Fire manifests as heat in the body and fire from the sun and so on in the outer world, and we have to go to great lengths to maintain this element within us, heating our houses, wearing clothes, and so on, along with taking in calories from food, which is of course this power of the sun stored within food.

With the element air, we can experience this in a direct way just by feeling into our breath. I really like this stage, as we have this direct experience of taking air into the body and releasing it back into the world: we cannot hang on to it, yet without it we would only last a few minutes.

The last of the elements are a little more difficult to understand, perhaps. Space can mean the space inside the body in contrast to the space outside of the body. It can also be understood as the space the body takes up in the world, and by extension we might like to consider the 'space' that our lives take up in the world: the places where we live, our possessions, such as clothes, books, cars, and so on. It is very interesting to realize that all the things we identify with and use to define us will on our death either be thrown or given away; other people will live in our houses and drive our cars. Sometimes this element is also associated with mobility – the fact that we move around, take up different spaces in the world, and that the space all around us allows this movement.

Lastly there is this element of consciousness, and this is the most difficult of the six to really understand. Traditionally we are often directed to notice all the various thoughts, feelings, images, sensations, and so on that are constantly arising in our minds, so in a way just being mindful of the contents of our consciousness. We can then ask ourselves: what are these experiences arising within? This stage is an opportunity to investigate the nature of consciousness itself. We should not expect a definitive answer – we just take an interest. We can also be aware that this 'element' that we call consciousness also exists in the outside world, in other people, animals, and so on. Traditionally some Buddhists see consciousness as existing in a kind of collective sense, a little like the idea of collective consciousness we find in the work of Jung. In traditional Buddhism, when we die the volitional nature of consciousness is such that it manifests again in another appropriate living being. I do not wish to go into this in any great detail, because I feel that what is most important in this stage, as with all of them, is to try and find a fixed sense of self in the element, and in doing so realize we can't, that they are in fact empty of any such selfhood.

I hope that gives you a sense of the practice. I think it is best to do it in not too tight a kind of way and be interested in what actually happens. It is a very rich practice that can take us into very interesting areas of contemplation and bring up a range of feelings. It is a strong practice too, so needs to be taken up with care. As with all meditation, do not push it – maintain a relaxed body and open attitude, be interested, and see what happens.

Of course today we have a different understanding of the elements from that of ancient India, but I hope it is not necessary to say that we do not have to take the practice in an overliteral way. It is the poetic nature of the practice that I think makes it so interesting, though it is still true that we are made of the same 'stuff' as everything else, and that this stuff is constantly moving, as it were, making up different things, manifesting in endless ways. But what is really being got at by this practice is not the nature of the elements, but rather our psychological clinging to them as 'us'.

In our terms, there is the possibility of 'seeing through' this clinging to a new perspective, one that understands our place in the world, not as a separate self-enclosed entity but rather as part of the warp and weave of all existence. This movement is difficult to achieve and even more difficult to sustain. It comes in flashes and is gone as soon as it appears. It might be experienced rather like a flash of lightning: for an instant everything is clear, and then, the next moment, everything is again plunged into the darkness of self-clinging. Or it may be that we glimpse something on the edge of our vision, an intimation that cannot be held on to. Although we cannot expect some sudden enduring breakthrough, there is nevertheless a slow dawning to a new way of being in the world brought about by sustained practice.

This change is not dependent upon dramatic experience with meditation. It might be that we do have such experiences, but even when and if they occur it is probably best not to make too much of them. James Hillman makes what I find a very useful distinction between what he calls 'events' and 'experience'. As so often with Hillman, he is using these terms in a somewhat idiosyncratic manner. Events refer to what happens to us; for example, we travel to India and see all these 'amazing' things, we take a lot of pictures on our iPhone, we rush from one location to another, we pack it in, we come home, then next year we go to some other exotic location. We go through life accumulating 'events', but between our trips we never really reflect on these events – we are always looking forward to the next trip. We might do the same sort of thing with lovers: we fall in love, we fall out of love, we fall in love again. We are caught up in a kind of psychic or emotional consumerism: our life is full of events, so we think we are living life to the full. We never sit around feeling a little depressed or melancholic, we never think about the past – we are living the 'now'. When we live like this, these amazing events just kind of rattle around inside of us – there is a constant hunger for more of them.

In contrast, we might not 'do' that much, but there is a reflective attitude, there is time in our lives to ruminate, to fully digest. We visit the same little Greek island for twenty years, we learn the language, we make connections with the family we stay with, we go to the weddings of their children whom we have seen grow up, we go to the rituals of moving the icons from one church to another, we learn how to cook the local cuisine. We go back again and feel sad that the family donkey has died in our absence. Well, I am laying it on a bit thick there, but you get the idea. In this way, the Greek island becomes part of us, it occupies a place in our psyche – we have a longing and a love for the smell of the herbs on the dry hillsides. What began as events start to become experiences: they are broken down and enter our bloodstream. Or it might also be that we only ever go once to the island, but we spend a lifetime remembering that trip: something happened there that stays with us, in our dreams, in our fantasies – it becomes part of us through reflection. In this way of looking at things, events have to be made into experience. The analogy of composting suggests itself, through which things return to earth, break down, and become incorporated into the ground of our being.

One of the ways we can consider meditation is as a kind of composting of events into experience. In meditation there is this establishment of stability, this construction of a vessel, through posture and the process of grounding, which allows the possibility of turning towards events, and this turning towards is also a turning over, a forking. It allows time for reflection and abiding: we stay with the events of our lives and they in turn and time begin to undergo some alchemical process – they are slowly turned into the gold of experience.

Our image of seeing through is related to this image of turning over, of allowing a kind of heat to build up in the vessel of our own bodies and minds. And this alchemical image is related in turn to that of repetition, of distilling and transforming through a long process of attending to with care. There are of course many ways in which we can attend with care to our experience (here I am using the term 'experience' in a more usual sense once again); meditation is just one way, but I think potentially a very important and effective one.

Sometimes, when we go to a major retrospective of an artist, we see that there are certain themes that seem to reappear over many decades. We also find this with many writers: they reuse the same elements again and again, look at the same things from a different perspective – there is a development, but there is also a fidelity to certain motifs or ideas that turn up over and over again. What we find is not a linear progression, but one full of regressions and looking again. We might find the same sort of thing in our meditation: we think we have 'dealt' with something, we have sussed it out, then there it is again. This can sometimes be a little disheartening: we feel that there is no progression, we are back where we started from, the same old stuff going round and round. But the psyche does not conform to the wishes of the ego; it does not recognize the machine time that measures out our daily lives; it does not proceed in a linear manner, but rather meanders like an old river, forms oxbow lakes that separate from the currents of flow of our conscious lives, lying still and torpid for years until we retrace our steps and return to them.

Earlier we had the poem 'A scattering', in which we encountered the image of elephants picking over the bones of their dead. The poet invites the spirit of the elephants to help him find 'new, hopeful arrangements' for his own sad thoughts. I mention this again because it implies that there is the possibility of rearranging, of finding new patterns in the old bones of our lives. And in this picking over is the possibility of seeing through, of making something new of what seemed once dead and buried.

Chapter twelve

The gateway of suffering

There is a very well-known story in the Buddhist tradition of a mother who has lost her only child. Here is a version of the story that has a rather interesting beginning often omitted in other tellings of the tale, normally known as the 'mustard seed' story.

> There was a rich man who found his gold suddenly transformed into ashes; and he took to his bed and refused all food. A friend, hearing of his sickness, visited the rich man and learned the cause of his grief. And the friend said: 'Thou didst not make good use of thy wealth. When thou didst hoard it up it was not better than ashes. Now heed my advice. Spread mats in the bazaar; pile up these ashes, and pretend to trade with them.' The rich man did as his friend had told him, and when his neighbours asked him, 'Why sellest thou ashes?' he said: 'I offer my goods for sale.'
>
> After some time a young girl, named Kisa Gotami, an orphan and very poor, passed by, and seeing the rich man in the bazaar, said: 'My lord, why pilest thou thus up gold and silver for sale?' And the rich man said: 'Wilt thou please hand me that gold and silver?' And Kisa Gotami took up a handful of ashes, and lo! they changed back into gold. Considering that Kisa Gotami had the mental eye of spiritual knowledge and saw the real worth of things, the rich man gave her in marriage to his son, and he said: 'With many, gold is no better than ashes, but with Kisa Gotami ashes become pure gold.'
>
> And Kisa Gotami had an only son, and he died. In her grief she carried the dead child to all her neighbours, asking them for medicine, and the people said: 'She has lost her senses. The boy is dead.' At length Kisa Gotami

met a man who replied to her request: 'I cannot give thee medicine for thy child, but I know a physician who can.' The girl said: 'Pray tell me, sir; who is it?' And the man replied: 'Go to Sakyamuni, the Buddha.'

Kisa Gotami repaired to the Buddha and cried: 'Lord and Master, give me the medicine that will cure my boy.' The Buddha answered: 'I want a handful of mustard-seed.' And when the girl in her joy promised to procure it, the Buddha added: 'The mustard-seed must be taken from a house where no one has lost a child, husband, parent, or friend.' Poor Kisa Gotami now went from house to house, and the people pitied her and said: 'Here is mustard-seed; take it!' But when she asked 'Did a son or daughter, a father or mother, die in your family?' They answered her: 'Alas the living are few, but the dead are many. Do not remind us of our deepest grief.' And there was no house but some beloved one had died in it.

Kisa Gotami became weary and hopeless, and sat down at the wayside, watching the lights of the city, as they flickered up and were extinguished again. At last the darkness of the night reigned everywhere. And she considered the fate of men, that their lives flicker up and are extinguished. And she thought to herself: 'How selfish am I in my grief! Death is common to all; yet in this valley of desolation there is a path that leads him to immortality who has surrendered all selfishness.'

Putting away the selfishness of her affection for her child, Kisa Gotami had the dead body buried in the forest. Returning to the Buddha, she took refuge in him and found comfort in the Dharma, which is a balm that will soothe all the pains of our troubled hearts.

The Buddha said: 'The life of mortals in this world is troubled and brief and combined with pain. For there is not any means by which those that have been born can avoid dying; after reaching old age there is death; of such a nature are living beings. As ripe fruits are early in danger of falling, so mortals when born are always in danger of death. As all earthen vessels made by the potter

The Myth of Meditation

end in being broken, so is the life of mortals. Both young and adult, both those who are fools and those who are wise, all fall into the power of death; all are subject to death.

'Of those who, overcome by death, depart from life, a father cannot save his son, nor kinsmen their relations. Mark I while relatives are looking on and lamenting deeply, one by one mortals are carried off, like an ox that is led to the slaughter. So the world is afflicted with death and decay, therefore the wise do not grieve, knowing the terms of the world. In whatever manner people think a thing will come to pass, it is often different when it happens, and great is the disappointment; see, such are the terms of the world.'[32]

Although the story is a little pat in some ways, the process of coming to terms with grief is symbolized by the woman having to go from door to door, having to repeat this looking for the mustard seed until the universal nature of her experience begins to dawn on her. Here we have an essential element of what we are calling seeing through. What was at first purely a personal loss takes on a new frame of reference: it is seen through different eyes, eyes that can now see the personal as an expression of something that is also a universal experience. It would be trite to claim that such a revisiting eradicates the grief, that the grief has been buried along with the body of the lost child; it might even be in some sense an intensification of the grief, but something very important has happened. What once separated us, cut us off from the world, now brings us into relationship with the world.

There is a need to move from a pain that separates us from others to a sorrow that connects us to others. However, even this is not enough. There is a desperate need not only to come into relationship with others, through personal events being made into experience that recognizes their universal nature, but also to take on the universal as personal. Here is an extract from *Ecopsychology*, by Joanna Macy:

Until the late twentieth century, every generation throughout history lived with the tacit certainty that there would be generations to follow. Each assumed, without questioning, that its children and children's children would walk the same Earth, under the same sky. Hardships, failures, and personal death were encompassed in that vaster assurance of continuity. That certainty is now lost to us, whatever our politics. That loss, unmeasured and immeasurable, is the pivotal psychological reality of our time.

The responses that arise from that reality are compounded by many feelings. There is terror at the thought of the suffering in store for our loved ones and others. There is rage that we live our lives under the threat of so avoidable and meaningless an end to the human enterprise. There is guilt; for as members of society we feel implicated in this catastrophe and haunted by the thought that we should be able to avert it. Above all, there is sorrow. Confronting so vast and final a loss as this brings sadness beyond the telling.

Even these terms, however – anger, fear, sorrow – are inadequate to convey the feelings we experience in this context. They connote emotions long familiar to our species as it has faced the inevitability of personal death. But the feelings that assail us now cannot be equated with dread of our own individual demise. Their source lies less in concerns for the personal self than in apprehensions of collective suffering – of what happens to others, to human life and fellow species, to the heritage we share, to the unborn generations to come, and to our blue-green planet itself, wheeling in space.

What we are really dealing with here is akin to the original meaning of compassion: 'suffering with'. It is the distress we feel in connection with the larger whole of which we are a part. It is our pain for the world.[33]

Macy, who is a Buddhist system theorist and eloquent spokesperson for the world, here voices the dreadful need that now faces us. Just as we tend to turn away from our own suffering, so we tend to turn away from the planetary distress we are now, if we are turned towards, faced with. But, although Macy rightly points out that this environmental situation that faces us is unequalled in human history, the understanding that we need to cultivate is not at all new. Indeed we might even suggest that it is a 'natural' perspective that has been lost, or rather hidden under an increasing emphasis on the individual ego perspective. When we look, for instance, at the culture of the 'primitive' Aboriginal people of Australia, we find an incredible sense of connection and responsibility towards the earth. Not only do they have an intimate and pragmatic knowledge of all that is around them, they also have a deep imaginative connection with their world. They feel themselves responsible for the world's continuation, which has to be sustained through 'dreaming', has to kept alive through the telling of stories, dance, and music as well as walking and 'dreaming' the earth. This kind of relationship to the world, a relationship that is fostered in the depths of the individual and collective psyche, is increasingly lost to modern life. We now dream of winning the lottery or getting a new car, rather than of our totem animals or features of the landscape for which we have the duty of care. Our dreams no longer sustain the world, but add to its destruction as a liveable environment for us and other life.

We saw in the story of Persephone the need for descent, and this too is part of the process by which we can reconnect to our own soul and the world soul. Macy stresses the need to face the sorrow and distress that coming into full awareness of our present position will entail, arguing that only when we do so will we be able to find the courage to move out of denial and become effective agents for change.

Our connection with our own psyches or souls is only continuous through our connection to the world. The Hermetic principle 'as above so below' is pivotal to an understanding of soul, to the soul of the individual, in an imaginative sense, as well as to that of the *anima mundi* or world soul. Orast the psyche cannot be separated from the world without a loss of soul in the individual. This idea is so potent that it has even re-emerged in modern ecology and on the fringes of science in the form of James Lovelock's Gaia theory.

When we lose this understanding of our place in the cosmos, we lose our own sense of soul and fall into literalism and materialism. This 'fall' is indeed equivalent to the biblical fall: we are cast out of the world of connection and meaning. The condition of loss of soul is common among 'primitive' people, where it betokens a loss of connection to the tribe and ancestors, as well as a failure to feel part of the natural world. Its modern equivalent might be termed alienation or an extreme utilitarian attitude towards the world and others, where worth is experienced purely in relation to the ego's needs; it is then a psychopathic state. The world is simply a resource to be exploited. Here is a poem that explores the consequence of aspects of this attitude:

The moment
by Margaret Atwood

The moment when, after many years
of hard work and a long voyage
you stand in the centre of your room,
house, half-acre, square mile, island, country,
knowing at last how you got there,
and say, I own this,
is the same moment when the trees unloose
their soft arms from around you,
the birds take back their language,
the cliffs fissure and collapse,
the air moves back from you like a wave
and you can't breathe.
No, they whisper. You own nothing.
You were a visitor, time after time
climbing the hill, planting the flag, proclaiming.
We never belonged to you.
You never found us.
It was always the other way round.[34]

This wish to claim the world as ours stems from a basic fear. At its root, it is a failure to confront our own vulnerability, coupled with a loss of a sense of belonging in the world.

As we saw in Part 1 on grounding, one of the most important things we are trying to bring about through our practice is a sense that the earth supports us, that we belong in the world, rather than in the bubble of a disembodied and frightened ego, constantly trying to shore itself up and maintain itself against the world. The movement from this isolated state to one of belonging and feeling at ease in our own skin and our own world is brought about through turning towards ourselves in all of our aspects; this in turn leads to a seeing through, in which we start to have a felt sense of 'being' in the world. Here is a simple practice that has been inspired by Bill Neidjie's *Story about Feeling*, which recounts his 'dreamings' as an Aboriginal elder.

Prayer to the world meditation

As always, take your time to set up the posture, relax, and come to the feeling of your breath in your body. Notice the sensations in your buttocks and legs that are arising due to their contact with the floor.

Have a sense that, wherever you happen to be, under you is the earth. Encourage the sense that the earth is supporting you; it supports you just as you are – happy or sad, relaxed or tense, calm or anxious, it still supports you. Know that this earth has done this all your life and has never asked anything from you in return.

Then have a sense of what is about you. You are probably in a room, but, wherever you happen to be, the sky is above you. This is the basic situation whenever you sit. The supportive earth below and the sheltering sky above. This is your heritage and can never be taken from you. If you are inside, have a sense of the building around you, a sense that this too is 'working' for you, provides you with shelter. So begin to be aware of what is there around you: the building and then what is outside of the building, the world around you. Perhaps you know there are some trees not far away; have a sense of those, know that these trees or grass are also working for you, processing the air that you breathe, maintaining life.

Notice whatever comes into awareness: it might be the feeling of your clothes against your skin – even these, which have some way or another come from the world, are working for you. The earth is working for you, the sky is working for you; the buildings, the roads, the trees and plants, even the sun and the stars, the moon and the oceans, the rivers and rain – it is all working for you, all maintaining your life in one way or another. Open the heart as it naturally unfolds, while staying aware of your breath. Your breath is working for you and provides a felt connection to the world.

Open the heart and the imagination; let the practice be a prayer to the world, an expression of gratitude to the world. Try to allow a sense that this is 'my' world arising in you and you are the world. Have a sense that, just as the whole world, the whole cosmos supports you, so you support the world. Let yourself feel your gratitude and responsibility as mutually supportive. Do not make it into a burden: support the world as the world supports you; know that this is how it is. Just as a tree is working for the world, so you are working for the world: this is just how things are, and it does not need to be felt as a weight, rather as a joy and an honour.

This is a very simple kind of practice, and what I have suggested above is just to give you a few ideas. Make it your own: follow your own imagination within the basic frame of turning towards the world, opening to the world, and cultivating a sense of gratitude towards the world. We have not left grounding behind, but rather are trying to begin to draw out the seeing through or 'insight' aspects a little more directly.

Chapter thirteen

....

The other side of insight

In the Buddhist tradition, 'insight' is a seeing through of what is termed *avidyā* (Sanskrit), normally translated as either 'ignorance' or 'delusion'. In early Buddhism, this was often explained as a failure to apprehend the full significance of the four noble truths: that of suffering, the cause of suffering, the end of suffering, and the path leading to the end of suffering. As an image, ignorance is often represented as a blind man or a man wearing a blindfold. We find this image as the 'first' of the twelve links of conditionality depicted around the outer rim of the Buddhist Wheel of Life. I say 'first', but of course it is a wheel, so there is no beginning. However, it is understood as the first link of this present life, in that it relates to the consciousness that operates between death and rebecoming. The next link is shown as a potter on a wheel building a pot, so this consciousness leads to the rebuilding of another life.

I am not here going to go into the metaphysical ramifications of this idea of rebecoming or reincarnation, as it is often wrongly called – wrongly because this implies that there is a 'something' that reincarnates. This is not the Buddhist understanding, where there is only a volitional energy that cannot be understood as a thing; there is no person getting reborn. Anyway, let's not go there. It is interesting to me that in beginners' classes this subject, that of rebirth, is perhaps the most popular. People want to know what happens to them when they die, which is fair enough, but they are often more interested in this than in how they might improve the lives they actually have. Often, they are a little surprised that I am not really that keen to discuss it, surprised perhaps when I tell them, 'I don't know', and instead encourage them to understand what Buddhism is trying to get at, which really is quite subtle and hard to grasp, and is better understood in a metaphorical sense – after all, it is metaphysics.

But the image of the blind man does interest me, or rather the image of the blindfolded man. His hands are usually free, so he could reach up and remove the blindfold: the blindness is not congenital. The question becomes: does the man know he is wearing a blindfold? There is this Tibetan saying I am very fond of, 'You cannot wake a man who is pretending to be asleep.' So this ignorance seems to be to some degree wilful. *Avidyā* is a negation of *vidyā*, which comes from a root meaning 'to see', so it has the literal sense of 'not to see'. It is then a blindness, or perhaps a turning away.

In later Buddhism, it becomes more common to talk about insight in terms of seeing into reality directly, seeing things as they really are. This means in particular seeing all things as bearing the so-called three marks we have already mentioned, those of unsatisfactoriness, insubstantiality, and impermanence. It is the seeing through to these fundamental characteristics of all things that gives rise to insight. When this is talked about in contemporary accounts of Buddhism, we are often given some examples from nature: we are asked to imagine a leaf falling from a tree, or some other such bucolic image. However, early Buddhism was a lot more direct, and had practices such as contemplating the decomposition of a human corpse. I think this points to an interesting inclination of our modern culture in relation to traditional beliefs: it is as if we want to make them all acceptable to our rather sentimental New Age sensibilities. More importantly, the traditional images direct us towards trying to realize these things not just as characteristic of 'nature', but rather as most fully revealed in our own bodies and experience. It is a little ironic to try and hold these marks at arm's length: what we need to do is to confront them as they manifest in us.

The main reason why I have over my years of teaching emphasized the body more and more is that it is in the body that we have the most direct access to impermanence and the other characteristics of reality. When we talk of reality, we often seem to have an unconscious tendency to see it as something out there, outside of us. We can see this happening on an emotional

The Myth of Meditation

level: while we are aware that all living things die, we never really accept that this truth applies to us. We know it, but at the same time we don't really see it. I am often struck these days when there is a new medical breakthrough reported in the news, a new cure for some disease or other: there seems to be a view underlying these reports that death is an unnatural and avoidable event. Of course I welcome genuine advances in medical science, but it does not matter how many breakthroughs there might be, we are still all going to die. Sometimes it might be better to pay more attention to what we do with our lives while we have them rather than being obsessed with prolonging life as long as 'humanly' possible – sometimes, it seems, with no regard for the quality of that life. Well, perhaps this is just a rationalization for my 'bad' habits.

The important point is that we need to realize the nature of reality within ourselves, not in the abstract. In this sense, we can say that insight is gained through the body, and, as I have been at pains to make clear, I do not mean body as opposed to mind, but rather body as including mind. Our physical body is a metaphor for our psychic body, or perhaps we should say the psyche often expresses itself through the physical body. In addition, the literal body is a gateway into the psyche. What is very clear is that a purely intellectual insight into reality is not sufficient. This does not mean it is of no use to us – it is a start, and perhaps even necessary as part of a deeper seeing into.

One of the things that we have to combat in our present culture is that it offers little support for this kind of work. We have on the one hand this rationalistic, scientific, materialistic culture that gives little room for the metaphorical imagination, and on the other the often superficial self-help, New Age culture that would have us believe that the universe is just waiting to fulfil all our 'dreams', that all we have to do is ask.

It is hard to sustain a practice on your own, without support. This has always been the case, and is one of the reasons why many spiritual traditions stress community and fellowship. In Buddhism this is known as 'sangha' and is regarded as one of the Three Jewels, along with the Buddha and the teachings. So it is seen as at the very heart of trying to cultivate 'insight', and, without it, the going is going to be very hard indeed. But this might also point to something else, something related. It might suggest that practice itself is more effective with others, that practising alone in your room lacks a certain potential that may be there when you practise with others. I teach a lot of retreats, and these days what I find most interesting about this is to try and work with what we might call the collective energy. I ask people to try and bear in mind that they are sitting with others, and to imagine that they are practising as much for them as they are for themselves, and also to imagine that the other people are practising for them. So here we have a similar image to the one we were trying to encourage with our last meditation practice: that of offering support and being supported. We might also recognize here what we have already talked about as the bodhisattva ideal, but brought down to a tangible level. I don't know what you can do about this if you are just trying to practise on your own. I would recommend that you try and find a human context that can help sustain you, if you can. If you cannot, you can at least imagine that you are engaging in this practice as much for others as for yourself.

In the end, whether you are practising alone or with others, insight as a sustained experience rather than as an 'event' normally takes a long time and a lot of practice, but really this does not matter.

Ithaka
by Constantine P. Cavafy

When you set out for Ithaka
ask that your way be long,
full of adventure, full of instruction.
The Laistrygonians and the Cyclops,
angry Poseidon – do not fear them:
such as these you will never find
as long as your thought is lofty, as long as a rare
emotion touch your spirit and your body.
The Laistrygonians and the Cyclops,
angry Poseidon – you will not meet them
unless you carry them in your soul,
unless your soul raise them up before you.

Ask that your way be long.
At many a Summer dawn to enter
with what gratitude, what joy –
ports seen for the first time;
to stop at Phoenician trading centres,
and to buy good merchandise,
mother of pearl and coral, amber and ebony,
and sensuous perfumes of every kind,
sensuous perfumes as lavishly as you can;
to visit many Egyptian cities,
to gather stores of knowledge from the learned.

Have Ithaka always in your mind.
Your arrival there is what you are destined for.
But don't in the least hurry the journey.
Better it last for years,
so that when you reach the island you are old,
rich with all you have gained on the way,
not expecting Ithaka to give you wealth.
Ithaka gave you a splendid journey.
Without her you would not have set out.
She hasn't anything else to give you.

And if you find her poor, Ithaka hasn't deceived you.
So wise you have become, of such experience,
that already you'll have understood what these Ithakas
     mean.[35]

In our journey, we might not keep a lofty spirit and welcome meeting the mythical monsters that for good or bad we all carry in our souls. We do not have to seek them out: if we sit in a relaxed way and turn repeatedly and with kindness towards the full range of our experience, including sensations, feelings, images, and thoughts, they will in their own time make themselves known. We do not have to force the practice; the unconscious does not respond to the will of the ego. The question then arises: what do we do when difficult material does arise?

In traditional Buddhism, we are given antidotes to what are termed 'hindrances'. These are commonly grouped into five categories: two pairs of opposites – hatred and desire, and restlessness and sloth – as well as doubt, which is understood as underlying the other four. The 'antidotes' to these hindrances range from suppression to open acceptance. I am not that keen on this particular teaching these days. It seems to me that it encourages a 'problematic' relationship to meditation. Apart from suppression, which certainly should be used with great circumspection, all the other antidotes really boil down to awareness. In the end, all we can really do is to be aware of what is happening. On the subject of suppression, I do think that there is one case in which this should be employed: that of physical restlessness – we do need to learn to sit still. Its mental companion of anxiety is often expressed through the body in fidgeting and general restlessness, so we will tend to stay unaware of our anxiety as long as it is being dissipated through this physical restlessness.

In our 'method' of practice, we are not really trying to get rid of anything, rather we are trying to turn towards our experience as fully and lovingly as we can. In order to do this, we have seen that there needs to be a stability established through the posture, the process of grounding, and attending to the breath. If these fundamentals are in place, we will be able to sit with whatever comes up in our practice, so when we lose our way we come back to the basics of posture and breath. We do this in a gentle and loving way, staying aware of whatever else is happening. We do not use this coming back as a way of escaping from what we might find difficult, or else even this coming back might in reality be a turning away.

Our way of working with the material is then to abide with it. Ideally we are just letting it be: we are interested in it, but we are not trying to manipulate it, get rid of it, or hold on to it. As I mentioned right at the beginning of this book, we will fail in this to some degree or other nearly all of the time, and that is okay – it is just what is, and we need to accept this with as much grace and humour as we can.

On occasion, it might be that what comes up is just too raw, too painful to turn towards – 'There are knocks in life so hard...' At these times, we might just not be ready to turn towards, and

The Myth of Meditation

we need to accept this, not force things. Emotions like loss and grief have their own time – they need to be respected, just as, in everyday life, there are some situations we just need to walk away from because we know that we cannot handle them at that time, and to try and do so could lead to dire consequences. I have had times in the past when, under serious emotional stress, I knew that I would 'lose it' if I did not walk away. When we are unable to sit with our dark materials, well we might just need to get up and do something else – go for a walk perhaps.

One thing I have found useful at such times is to chant. Chanting is a very central practice to some schools of Buddhism: it has the advantage of being active, and so we can engage with it even when other forms of practice seem impossible to us. In periods when life has been hard, I have often made chanting the mainstay of my practice.

Most mantras in Buddhism relate to particular archetypal Buddhist figures, such as Green Tārā, whom we met earlier. They are often a form of their name, as in the case of Green Tārā, whose mantra is *oṃ tāre tuttāre ture svāhā*. It is best if possible to chant these mantras out loud, and it is easy to find versions of them chanted on the Internet. Traditionally they are often chanted 108 times, which in the case of this one will take about 15 minutes. It really is a very effective practice if you are feeling too fragile to meditate in the manner we have been considering. I often also chant at the beginning of a meditation, as it is a great way to come into the body: it both regulates the breath and brings energy and aliveness to the body. I do a lot of chanting on retreat, as it is a wonderful collective practice and can foster a real sense of practising together and supporting one another, which is somewhat harder to do through silent practice. I do highly recommend it for everyone as part of their practice. It clearly is strengthened if you have a feeling and connection with the figure whose mantra you are chanting, but, even if you do not, it will still have a good effect, and might also lead you to wanting to find out more about the figure.

So at those times when staying with our raw experience feels too painful and yet we want to find a way to maintain a connection with our practice, chanting is one way. However, I think there is something more fundamental we can do, which is to understand our practice in such a way that it includes those periods when formal practice does not seem to be open to us. We could evoke an organic metaphor here: sometimes we need to let things lie fallow. There are times when we have to trust in the soul and leave well alone. If we think of meditation as something that should make us feel a certain way, it is very hard to sit when we feel bad. But there is perhaps a way we can look at meditation that makes it possible to sit with even the most difficult states. This I would suggest is the perspective of what we have been calling soul.

Very often our motivation to meditate is driven by our ego. This is not a 'bad' thing – it is just how it is. However, when we are motivated by an idea of improving ourselves, this will at some point prove to have limitations. The motivations of the ego are often at odds with the soul's needs. When we try to impose ideas such as integration, positivity, insight, purification, and enlightenment on to the soul, it will shrink away, for the soul is unable to stand too much light. The soul needs melancholic periods and has its own time.

I think that one of the main pressures that we have both as individuals and collectively is the fantasy of continuous growth. This is based on a refusal to face up to the real nature of our lives. As meditators, we need to see through the naive notion that we have of growth. If we have a simplistic idea of growth, this will leave no room for the regressions and serpentine nature of the psyche. Here we see the limitations of any particular image or metaphor that we might employ in order to try and make sense of what it is we are trying to do as meditators. For example, I have earlier in this book used the metaphor of the tree. The fantasy of growth implied by the tree is one that evokes the little acorn that grows into the mighty oak. This image of growth is teleological, the end result being given from the start. Moreover, the image tends to be a single tree existing in magnificent isolation. This image, while at times it may be useful and sustaining, may at other times become an image that oppresses us. It might feel like we are being nailed on to this tree, no longer a metaphor of growth but a cross to bear.

When we are dependent on any one image or indeed myth, in this case that of growth and ascent, we will be bemused when life drags us down, when Hades demands his due.

I think that this is an important point, as it is an inflexible attachment to a particular image or metaphor that leads to fanaticism, and we are all aware of the dangers of this, particularly when married to a 'spiritual' myth. This mono perspective is a psychological literalism, and is the primary enemy of a poetic or soulful approach to practice. A single vision, however glorious, will at some point cease to be a support, and instead become the very thing that stops us going deeper. For example, if our only perspective on meditation is the gaining of higher states, or achieving enlightenment, or thinking that it is all about seeing through, at some point this particular vision will let us down, or at least limit our self-awareness and wisdom.

James Hillman often reminded us that the gods do not appear alone – they are a bit like the London buses: they come in twos or threes, and even the individual god will have many faces. When there is only one stone-faced god, one understanding, one way of seeing, everything becomes literal. Our metaphors and images lose their fluidity, their playfulness; they dry out into hard facts. Enlightenment is no longer a fascinating jewel in which everything is reflected, but an objective state that must be attained, a mountain to be conquered. To understand that the gods are never alone even in their singularity is to see through literalism.

The current trend is to reduce meditation to mindfulness, and to frame this within a scientific and medical model. This has the initial advantage of making it appealing to many people who would not be attracted to meditation when understood as a religious practice. However, it is also limiting in its own way. It runs the risk of shutting down the imagination and reducing meditation to an adaptive intervention concerned only with the individual's well-being. When meditation is understood within its traditional Buddhist setting, it becomes a radical challenge to the values and norms of a society based on greed and exploitation of the planet. It challenges us to look deeply into our own self-identity and to redefine ourselves as belonging to life.

At the heart of meditation is the call to deep compassion and a life led in sympathy with all life – not yet another technique to feel a little bit better about ourselves as we carry on in an otherwise unchanged life. The radical change that meditation can support is based on a seeing through of the self-centred nature of our lives, and it is only by this kind of insight that we begin to increasingly experience ourselves as in the service of life, experiencing all life as something intimate and meaningful.

> may my heart always be open to little
> *by ee cummings*
>
> may my heart always be open to little
> birds who are the secrets of living
> whatever they sing is better than to know
> and if men should not hear them men are old
>
> may my mind stroll about hungry
> and fearless and thirsty and supple
> and even if it's sunday may i be wrong
> for whenever men are right they are not young
>
> and may myself do nothing usefully
> and love yourself so more than truly
> there's never been quite such a fool who could fail
> pulling all the sky over him with one smile[36]

Notes and references

1 James Hillman, *Revisioning Psychology*, Harper & Row, New York 1975, p.68.
2 Robinson Jeffers, 'Carmel Point', in *The Collected Poetry of Robinson Jeffers, Three Volumes*, ed. Tim Hunt, Stanford University Press, Stanford, CA 1995.
3 *Saṃyutta Nikāya* 22.43, *Attadīpa Sutta: An Island to Oneself*, trans. Maurice O'Connell Walshe, available at https://www.accesstoinsight.org/tipitaka/sn/sn22/sn22.043.wlsh.html, accessed on 26 October 2018.
4 Wallace Stevens, 'Reply to Papini', in *The Collected Poems of Wallace Stevens*, Knopf, New York 1971, p.446.
5 *The Voice of the Buddha (Lalitavistara)*, trans. Gwendolyn Bays, 2 vols, Dharma Publishing, Berkeley, CA 1983, vol.2, pp.481–3.
6 Pablo Neruda, 'Keeping quiet', in *Extravaganza*, trans. Alastair Reid, Farrar, Straus and Giroux, New York 1974.
7 William Carlos Williams, 'Thursday', in *Collected Poems: Volume 1, 1909–1939*, ed. A. Walton Litz and Christopher MacGowan, Carcanet and New Directions Publishing, Manchester 1988.
8 Miroslav Holub, 'The door' (1962), trans. Ian Milner, in *Poems Before & After: Collected English Translations*, trans. Ian Milner, Jarmila Milner *et al.*, Bloodaxe, Hexham 2006.
9 In Hafiz, *The Gift*, trans. Daniel Ladinsky, Penguin Compass, London 1999, p.83.
10 Derek Walcott, 'Earth', in *Sea Grapes*, Farrar, Straus and Giroux, New York 1976.
11 Miroslav Holub, 'What the heart is like', trans. Ewald Osers, in *Poems Before & After*.
12 Christopher Reid, 'A scattering', in *A Scattering*, Arête Books, Denver, CO 2009.
13 *Dogen's Extensive Record: A Translation of the Eihei Koroku*, trans. Shohaku Okumura, Wisdom Publications, Somerville, MA 2005, p.132.
14 Francis Bacon, quoted in David Sylvester, *The Brutality of Fact: Interviews with Francis Bacon*, Thames & Hudson, London 1987, p.10.
15 Stephan Beyer, *The Cult of Tārā: Magic and Ritual in Tibet*, University of California Press, Berkeley, CA 1978.

16 César Vallejo, 'The black heralds', trans. Richard Schaaf and Kathleen Ross, *Latin American Literary Review Press* (1990).

17 *Saṃyutta Nikāya* 36.21, PTS S iv.230. Translated by Dhivan Thomas Jones, used with permission.

18 *Udana* 1.3.

19 In *The Three Jewels*, Windhorse Publications, Birmingham 1977, pp.69–70.

20 *Dhammapada*, trans. Daw Mya Tin, MA, available at https://tienvnguyen.net/images/file/kx6TZFiS0ggQAEMp/dhammapada-versesandstories-a.pdf, accessed on 26 October 2018.

21 Philip Larkin, 'This be the verse', in *Collected Poems*, Faber and Faber, London 1988. Philip Larkin, 'This be the verse', in *The Collected Poems of Philip Larkin*, edited by Archie Burnett, New York, Farrar, Straus and Giroux, 2012.

22 See https://sociopathicstyle.com/narcissistic-personality-disorder/, accessed on 26 October 2018.

23 Roger Keyes, 'Hokusai says', available at https://www.youtube.com/watch?v=I-_6K56uz-k, accessed on 26 October 2018.

24 In Gian Carlo Calza, 'Hokusai: a universe', in Gian Carlo Calza, Matthi Forrer, and Roger S. Keyes, *Hokusai*, Phaidon, New York 2004, p.7.

25 Derek Walcott, 'Love after love', in *Collected Poems, 1948–1984*, Faber and Faber, London 1986. Derek Walcott, 'Love after Love', in *The Poetry of Derek Walcott 1948-2013*, selected by Glyn Maxwell, New York, Farrar, Straus and Giroux, 2014.

26 Raymond Carver, 'Late fragment', in *A New Path to the Waterfall*, Grove Press/Atlantic Monthly Press/Curtis Brown, New York 1989.

27 Paramananda, *The Body*, Windhorse Publications, Birmingham 2007, pp.95–7.

28 W.H. Auden, 'Musée des beaux arts' (1938), in *Another Time*, Faber and Faber, London 1940.

29 Naomi Shihab Nye, 'Kindness', in *Words under the Words: Selected Poems by Naomi Shihab Nye*, Eighth Mountain Press, Portland, OR 1998.

30 Wilko Johnson, on *Front Row*, BBC Radio 4, 25 January 2013.

31 Wallace Stevens, 'Thirteen ways of looking at a blackbird', in *The Collected Poems of Wallace Stevens*, Faber and Faber, London 2006.

32 'The mustard seed', available at http://www.sacred-texts.com/bud/btg/btg85.htm, accessed on 26 October 2018.

33 Joanna Macy, 'Working through environmental despair', in *Ecopsychology*, ed. T. Roszak, M.E. Gomes, and A.D. Kanner, Sierra Club, New York 1995, pp.240–62 (241).

34 Margaret Atwood, 'The moment', in *Eating Fire*, Virago, London 1998.

35 Constantine P. Cavafy, 'Ithaka', trans. Edmund Keeley and Philip Sherrard, in *Collected Poems*, ed. George Savidis, Princeton University Press, Princeton, NJ 1992.

36 ee cummings, 'may my heart always be open to little', in *Complete Poems: 1904–1962*, ed. George J. Firmage, Liveright Publishing Corporation, New York 1991.

Index

Introductory Note

References such as '178–9' indicate (not necessarily continuous) discussion of a topic across a range of pages. Wherever possible in the case of topics with many references, these have either been divided into sub-topics or only the most significant discussions of the topic are listed. Because the entire work is about 'meditation', the use of this term (and certain others which occur constantly throughout the book) as an entry point has been minimised. Information will be found under the corresponding detailed topics.

engagement 34
enlightenment 8, 12, 15, 45, 59, 94, 102, 140–1
  European 23
events 108, 121–2, 127, 135–6
evil 15–16
exercises 22, 29–31, 34–5, 39–40, 45–6, 54, 65, 98
experience 30–3, 61–4, 66–8, 70–3, 79–82, 88–9, 116, 121–2
  actual 31, 33, 59, 68
  direct 6–7, 80, 89, 119
eyes 5, 16, 40, 86, 96, 103, 113, 127

failure 93, 105, 128, 130, 133
family 75, 78, 121, 126
fanaticism 15, 141
fantasy 3, 7, 21, 40, 53, 100–101, 122, 140
fathers 101–2, 116, 126–7
feet 22, 30, 33–6, 48, 65, 87–8, 103, 114
  of clay 37
  soles 22, 30, 87, 103
fidgeting 30, 138
food 35, 53, 60, 119, 125
friends 6, 22, 60, 97, 107, 125–6
Fuji, Mount 91

Gaia theory 41
garden 30, 79, 90
gateway of suffering 125–31
gift, The 44
goddesses 14–15, 85, 101
gods 3, 15–16, 74, 86, 101, 104, 141
good posture 19–27
gratitude to the world 132, 137
Green Tārā 74, 80, 102, 139
grief 16, 43, 58, 86, 101, 125–7, 139
grounding 33, 39, 41, 44–5, 51, 54, 58, 113
  as image 11–19
  process 122, 138
growth 15, 58, 76, 78, 140–1
guilt 17, 75, 128

Hades 101, 141
Hafiz 43–4
hair 13, 48, 118
happiness 77, 85
hatred 2, 59, 138
head 22–3, 29, 39, 46–7, 52–3, 63, 69, 86–8
heart 1–2, 5–6, 35–7, 50–2, 85–6, 88, 96–8, 142
  centre 53, 88
heat 119, 122
heaven 15, 91
Heidegger, Martin 16, 42, 73, 82
higher states 59, 67–8, 141
Hillman, James 3–4, 72, 117, 121, 141
history 2–3, 99, 101, 103–5, 107, 109, 111, 128–9
Hokusai says 90–2, 103

Holub, Miroslav 7, 40, 50–1
home 13, 61, 90, 121
hopelessness 43
hospices 1, 108

ignorance 59, 133–4
images 7, 11–13, 19–20, 57–8, 70, 96–7, 133–4, 140–1
  visual 7
imaginal ground 1
imagination 37, 41–2, 46, 51–2, 72–3, 88–9, 96, 132
imaginative relationship 41, 64
imagining, light 30, 46, 52, 88
imbalance 4, 63
imperfection 94
in-breath 46, 52, 88
insight 23, 34, 49, 51, 59, 105, 108
  other side of 133–41
intellect 23, 103, 116
interpenetration 23, 37, 47
intimacy 4, 15, 17, 49, 61, 92–3
islands 6, 121–2, 130, 137
Ithaka 136–7

Jeffers, Robinson 4
Johnson, Wilko 109
Jove 82
joy 2, 44, 68, 77, 91, 126, 132, 137
Juno 85

karma 75–7
karma niyama 77
Keyes, Roger 90
kindness 19, 97, 106–7, 137
kindness and care, call to 73–83
Kisa Gotami 125–6
knees 22, 48, 87

Laistrygonians 136
language 1–3, 25, 36, 94, 97, 121, 130
Larkin, Philip 81
Late fragment 95
legs 22, 87–8, 105, 131
  lower 87
  upper 22, 88
liberation 43–4, 102
life 53–4, 58–60, 73–5, 89–100, 108–9, 115–16, 131–3, 141–2
  aliveness in 85, 87, 89, 91, 93, 95, 97
  Buddha's 53, 59–60
  daily 99–100, 106
  everyday 44, 139
  spiritual 21, 54
light 2, 4, 6, 44, 52, 89, 101, 108
light imagining 30, 46, 52, 88
linear progression 58, 122
listening 20, 40, 96
literalism 14, 117, 130, 141
loss 3, 16, 58, 72, 93, 128, 130, 139

upright position 22–3, 29
utu niyama 76

Vallejo, César 74
visual images 7
voices 14, 40, 79, 85–6, 107, 128
volitional mental order 77
vulnerability 4, 130

wabi-sabi 93–5
Walcott, Derek 48, 92–3
water 86, 90, 106, 118–19
water spirit 86
weight 30, 33, 40, 65, 102, 108, 118, 132

Western tradition 23, 37, 108
What the heart is like 50–1
willed actions 75–6
Williams, William Carlos 32–4, 82
windows 18, 104, 107, 114
winter 101–2
wisdom 2, 49, 82, 102–3, 141
women 18, 23, 114, 127
woods 14, 85–6, 90, 104
words 6, 8, 33, 36, 91–2, 94–5, 108, 117
world, natural 16–17, 130
world soul 41, 129
worry 18, 21, 30, 35, 46, 59, 65, 70

Zen Mind, Beginner's Mind 69
Zen sickness 46
Zeus 101

WINDHORSE PUBLICATIONS

Windhorse Publications is a Buddhist charitable company based in the UK. We place great emphasis on producing books of high quality that are accessible and relevant to those interested in Buddhism at whatever level. We are the main publisher of the works of Sangharakshita, the founder of the Triratna Buddhist Order and Community. Our books draw on the whole range of the Buddhist tradition, including translations of traditional texts, commentaries, books that make links with contemporary culture and ways of life, biographies of Buddhists, and works on meditation.

As a not-for-profit enterprise, we ensure that all surplus income is invested in new books and improved production methods, to better communicate Buddhism in the 21st century. We welcome donations to help us continue our work – to find out more, go to windhorsepublications.com.

The Windhorse is a mythical animal that flies over the earth carrying on its back three precious jewels, bringing these invaluable gifts to all humanity: the Buddha (the 'awakened one'), his teaching, and the community of all his followers.

Windhorse Publications	Perseus Distribution	Windhorse Books
17e Sturton Street	210 American Drive	PO Box 574
Cambridge CB1 2SN	Jackson TN 38301	Newtown NSW 2042
UK	USA	Australia

info@windhorsepublications.com

THE TRIRATNA BUDDHIST COMMUNITY

Windhorse Publications is a part of the Triratna Buddhist Community, an international movement with centres in Europe, India, North and South America and Australasia. At these centres, members of the Triratna Buddhist Order offer classes in meditation and Buddhism. Activities of the Triratna Community also include retreat centres, residential spiritual communities, ethical Right Livelihood businesses, and the Karuna Trust, a UK fundraising charity that supports social welfare projects in the slums and villages of India.

Through these and other activities, Triratna is developing a unique approach to Buddhism, not simply as a philosophy and a set of techniques, but as a creatively directed way of life for all people living in the conditions of the modern world.

If you would like more information about Triratna please visit thebuddhistcentre.com or write to:

London Buddhist Centre	Aryaloka	Sydney Buddhist Centre
51 Roman Road	14 Heartwood Circle	24 Enmore Road
London E2 0HU	Newmarket NH 03857	Sydney NSW 2042
UK	USA	Australia

ALSO BY PARAMANANDA

Change Your Mind

Paramananda

An accessible and thorough guide, this best-seller introduces two Buddhist meditations and deals imaginatively with practical difficulties, meeting distraction and doubt with determination and humour.

Inspiring, calming and friendly ... If you've always thought meditation might be a good idea, but found other step-by-step guides lacking in spirit, this book could finally get you going. — *Here's Health*

ISBN 9781 899579 75 4
£9.99 / $13.95 / €12.95
208 pages

A Deeper Beauty: Buddhist Reflections on Everyday Life

Paramananda

The best-selling author of *Change Your Mind* suggests ways of uncovering meaning, depth and stillness in lives often fuelled by activity and bombarded with information. Using reflections and stories from his own life, he discusses themes such as poetry, death, joy and imagination, offering courage and kindness in the search for meaning.

ISBN 9781 899579 44 0
£10.99 / $16.95 / €13.95
208 pages

The Buddha's Noble Eightfold Path

Sangharakshita

The Noble Eightfold Path is the most widely known of the Buddha's teachings. It is ancient, extending back to the Buddha's first discourse and is highly valued as a unique treasury of wisdom and practical guidance on how to live our lives.

This introduction takes the reader deeper while always remaining practical, inspiring and accessible. Sangharakshita translates ancient teachings and makes them relevant to the way we live our lives today.

Probably the best 'life coaching' manual you'll ever read, the key to living with clarity and awareness. – Karen Robinson, *The Sunday Times*

ISBN 9781 899579 81 5
£9.99 / $13.95 / €12.95
176 pages

The Art of Reflection

Ratnaguna

It is all too easy either to think obsessively, or to not think enough. But how do we think usefully? How do we reflect? Like any art, reflection can be learnt and developed, leading to a deeper understanding of life and to the fullness of wisdom. *The Art of Reflection* is a practical guide to reflection as a spiritual practice, about 'what we think and how we think about it'. It is a book about contemplation and insight, and reflection as a way to discover the truth.

This is a gem of a book that can be savoured and will enlighten. – Professor Paul Gilbert, author of *The Compassionate Mind*

No-one who takes seriously the study and practice of the Dharma should fail to read this ground-breaking book. – Sangharakshita, founder of the Triratna Buddhist Community

'The Art of Reflection' *will give teachers insight into Buddhist practice. Even more importantly, it may help to develop the ability to engage in deeper personal and professional reflection.*
– Joyce Miller, *REtoday*

ISBN 9781 899579 89 1
£9.99 / $16.95 / €12.95
160 pages

Not About Being Good: A Practical Guide to Buddhist Ethics

Subhadramati

While there are numerous books on Buddhist meditation and philosophy, there are few books that are entirely devoted to the practice of Buddhist ethics. Subhadramati communicates clearly both their founding principles and the practical methods to embody them.

Buddhist ethics are not about conforming to a set of conventions, not about 'being good' in order to gain rewards. Instead, living ethically springs from the awareness that other people are no different from yourself. You can actively develop this awareness, through cultivating love, clarity and contentment. Helping you to come into greater harmony with all that lives, this is ultimately your guidebook to a more satisfactory life.

In touch with the wonder of being alive, Subhadramati is a realistic and sympathetic guide to ethics in the twenty-first century. – Vidyamala Burch, author of *Mindfulness for Health*

Writing with passion, humour and delicacy, gloriously free from moralism, her aim is to help us live a richer and fuller life. – Maitreyabandhu, author of *Life with Full Attention*

Places ethics and meditation at the heart of Buddhist practice, and shows how they work together in transforming ordinary human beings into Buddhas. – Professor Damien Keown, author of *The Nature of Buddhist Ethics*

1SBN: 9781 909314 01 6
£9.99 / $16.95 / €12.95
176 pages

The Buddha on Wall Street: What's Wrong with Capitalism and What We Can Do about It

Vaḍḍhaka Linn

After his Enlightenment the Buddha set out to help liberate the individual, and create a society free from suffering. The economic resources now exist to offer a realistic possibility of providing everyone with decent food, shelter, work and leisure, to allow each of us to fulfil our potential as human beings, whilst protecting the environment. What is it in the nature of modern capitalism which prevents that happening? Can Buddhism help us build something better than our current economic system, to reduce suffering and help the individual to freedom? In this thought-provoking work, Vaḍḍhaka Linn explores answers to these questions by examining our economic world from the moral standpoint established by the Buddha.

An original, insightful, and provocative evaluation of our economic situation today. If you wonder about the social implications of Buddhist teachings, this is an essential book. – David Loy, author *Money, Sex, War, Karma*

Lays bare the pernicious consequences of corporate capitalism and draws forth from Buddhism suggestions for creating benign alternatives conducive to true human flourishing. – Bhikkhu Bodhi, editor *In the Buddha's Words*

Questions any definition of wellbeing that does not rest on a firm ethical foundation, developing a refreshing Buddhist critique of the ends of economic activity. – Dominic Houlder, Adjunct Professor in Strategy and Entrepreneurship, London Business School

ISBN 978 1 909314 44 3
£9.99 / $16.99 / €12.95
272 pages

Free Time!: From Clock-Watching to Free-Flowing, a Buddhist Guide

Vajragupta Staunton

In our fast moving world many of us feel our time is wound tight, our lives constantly hassled and hectic. 'Fast-forward' seems to be the collective default setting. So often we can be over busy and over stimulated, and this can send stress levels higher and higher.

In *Free Time!*, Vajragupta Staunton shows us that investigating our experience of time, and considering our relationship with it, can be deeply and powerfully transformative. Noticing the feel and texture of our time can help us see more clearly, and understand more profoundly, the anxiety and restlessness that so often dominates our minds. We and time are intimately intertwined. It is not something we are in; it is something that we are. That means we have a choice about our experience of time: what we do with our minds and our hearts, with our thoughts and emotions, will condition the quality of the time we live in.

Today we're all familiar with time-stress – how can Buddhist practices help us cope with it? What does Buddhism have to teach us about our experience and understanding of time? Vajragupta's new book offers fresh perspectives on a problem that continues to worsen, and original ways to address it. – David Loy, author of *Money, Sex, War, Karma*

Refreshingly original, beautifully written, and crystal clear. I can't remember the last time I read a book that yielded so many insights. – Ratnaguna, author of *The Art of Reflection*

As someone who suffers from chronic, clock-watching, inbox-obsessing busyness, I found this a challenging, but ultimately inspiring, book. Hints for experiencing timelessness, and stories of both contemporary acquaintances and the life of the Buddha, make it all very human and accessible, firmly rooted in experience. – Sir David Spiegelhalter, Centre for Mathematical Sciences, University of Cambridge

ISBN 978 1 911407 23 2
£14.99 / $19.95 / €16.95
256 pages